22 Under 22

22 Under 22

Young People Speak!

Emma Harrington, Executive Editor

Editors:

Madelaine Formica

Abby Doty

Kayla Gray

Flexible Press

Minneapolis, Minnesota

2020

COPYRIGHT © 2020 Flexible Press
www.flexiblepub.com

ISBN 978-1-7339763-7-4

About Flexible Press: Flexible Press is dedicated to supporting authors, communities, and mission-driven non-profits through story. Somewhere between some and all of the profits from Flexible Press titles are donated to relevant nonprofits. Find out more at www.flexiblepub.com.

Copy Editor: Vicki Adang,
Mark My Words Editorial Services, LLC

Cover by Chad Lovejoy and Bob McNeil. Artist statement: "Through art in its many forms, Chad Lovejoy and Bob McNeil dedicate their work to one cause—justice."

Introduction

November 2019, I reached out to Flexible Press as a wide-eyed college sophomore seeking experience in the publishing industry. After an evening spent brainstorming in a coffee shop, the idea for an anthology highlighting young people's perspectives on politics, family, growing up in systems of oppression, and everything in between was born.

Little did we realize how crucial this perspective would become in the coming months. Since the start of the project, there has been a global pandemic, protests, and uprisings against police brutality, as well as an overall upheaval of what "normal" life seemed to be.

In a sense, *22 Under 22* comes at the perfect time. A time of change, of despair, of young people's resilience and bravery. It is more important than ever to center the voices of young people, BIPOC folks, folks with disabilities, women, and LGBT+ folks. We must listen to the younger generations as they heal from systems of oppression and write a new reality into existence.

—*Emma Harrington*
Executive Editor

The Suburbs in Crisis

"I tell ya, it's because they're so kissy-kissy," I overhear a woman spout to her friend. Her companion, dressed in a similar, yet not identical pair of purple leggings, nods in agreement. "Those Itaaalians," continues the first woman, flattening her A like a true New Yorker. "They have just such a . . . such a . . . what's the word? *Kissy-kissy* society." "I know!" responds the second. "Even *guys* kiss each other when they see other *guys*." The first woman's rather large dog begins pawing at the second woman's rather small dog. The women, who walk six feet apart from each other, ignore it. "That's why it's not gonna get that bad in America. We aren't as . . . kissy-kissy."

Worried they'll notice that I've slowed to listen in, I pick up my pace and continue on my run.

April days like these were always my favorite growing up— 68 degrees, sunny, cherry blossoms beginning to bloom. An avid runner, I've always taken advantage of this weather; by now, I've jogged nearly every sidewalk in this sleepy New Jersey suburb. I'm not used to having company.

Throughout my five-mile route, I dip and dive in an attempt to stay socially distanced from the small clusters of walkers that pepper the sidewalks. Running paths that usually lie untrodden now suffer from hesitant traffic jams as walkers, bikers, and joggers attempt to squeeze through narrow straightaways, silently maneuvering around each other as if surrounded by invisible force fields.

I pass family after family after family on group bike rides— the type of collective exercise usually reserved for only the most exemplar of suburban households. You know the type of family I'm talking about—they also eat gluten-free dinners.

I pass a sign that says, "Honk for Will's birthday." I wish I had a car.

I pass a father and his two young daughters drawing with colored chalk on their driveway. Actually, I pass a 30-year-old man furiously scribbling the final indigo strip of a rainbow, unwilling to abandon the project that his toddlers so easily dismissed.

When I turn down a particularly remote road, a woman cusping on old age wobbles passed me on a pair of roller blades. I smile at her. She offers back a grimace—a valiant effort to smile through her unease.

Throughout my run, I am engaged in a drawn-out race against a middle school bike gang. The preteens may whiz past me down hills, but on inclines I stride past the huffers and puffers at the back of the pack. The gaggle has to stop every half-mile because someone's gearshift isn't working, or someone's mom called, or most inconveniently, Jimmy needs another water break. Meanwhile, I, the tortoise, trudge steadily along.

*

A young man dressed in pajama bottoms and a Hook 'Em Horns T-shirt stands in the patch of grass in front of his house, tossing a ball into the air and catching it with the same hand. With his other, he holds a cellphone to his ear, "Yes, ma'am, I'm just calling to assure you that we are still a *fully* operational pharmacy and are doing free deliveries throughout the *entire* state of New Jersey." A pause. "Yes, ma'am, you heard that correctly: free, f-r-e-e, free medicine delivery straight to your door."

I do a double take as a Model T Ford–looking car sputters past me. An old man leans out the window and calls, "Isn't it a lovely day to take her for a spin?!?"

I watch two couples stop to chat as they pass each other on their respective daily walks. "Paul," one of the wives exclaims, interrupting her husband's animated sentence. "Six feet! Six feet!" Paul raises his hands to prove his innocence and takes an overexaggerated step back. He makes eye contact with the other man—*women*.

I pass a woman explaining to another woman—presumably her mother—that if you want to make iced coffee, you need to make your coffee stronger, like, much stronger, like, twice as strong, because the ice will dilute the coffee when it melts. The mother, who seems to have a basic understanding of how liquids work, purses her lips and silently absorbs the lesson. She must know her daughter's unnecessary explanation comes from a place of love, from concern for her mother's ability to adapt to life in this strange new world, especially to the lack of daily Starbucks.

This new world— the one filled with tricycles and middle-aged men on road bikes and people taking the time to enjoy the cherry blossoms—though strange, feels alive.

The world of stifled cities, goggle-shaped bruises, raspy breath, and lonely death is confined to the television. Like *Game of Thrones* and magic diet pills, it feels imagined.

I feel the virus only indirectly, through the precautions taken to curb its spread, rather than through the grief and pain it is wreaking around the world: my brother's quarantine beard, the uncomfortable tug of my too heavy hair that should've been cut weeks ago, and most disturbingly, through the eerie blossoming of my suburban community. When you have savings, being newly unemployed means an opportunity to enjoy the outdoors.

But even in Madison, the virus has started to slip beyond the screen.

On my jog, a woman shrieks at me for coming too close to her. Not a shriek of anger, but a shriek of fear—fear of me.

In my living room, I turn to see my mother take her temperature for what must be the fifteenth time since the start of the movie—it's *Amadeus* tonight. Spoiler: 39-year-old Mozart dies of strep throat at the end.

About halfway through, she goes to the kitchen to check her blood-oxygen levels. She ordered the toy-looking monitor on Amazon last week, the day after she heard her friend Alan died, a casualty of corona.

He was in the hospital for fourteen hours total, from start to death. He died alone.

*

In the morning, I log into Zoom for a class called Human Rights. We discuss the greatest atrocities in recent history—Rwanda, Bosnia, the Holocaust—and how the United States failed to prevent them, or didn't even try.

Next up, Zen Buddhism. We learn about the Blood Bowl—the blood-filled period hell that awaits women whose sons do not pray for them enough.

And then Chinese. This week our lesson is on government propaganda, specifically the media's coverage of a 2016 flood in Wuhan. The textbook was published last year.

And finally, journalism. We video call professors, government officials, reporters, analysts. From our respective living rooms, we discuss Viktor Orban's authoritarian power grab in Hungary, the Covid-19 outbreak on the *U.S.S. Theodore Roosevelt,* a Chinese woman in New York who had acid thrown in her face, the overwhelming waves of patients, the overwhelming wave of unemployment and domestic violence, the methods doctors use to choose which patient gets the last ventilator and which dies, Texas's decision to make abortion an elective surgery, how China is going to use the virus to justify authoritarianism, how other countries are going to follow, how this virus and the rally-around-the-flag effect that comes with it will likely be Trump's key to success in the next election, if it's worth broadcasting Trump on prime-time television, why the United States was so unprepared, how we could've been better prepared, who has died because we weren't, the vandalization of 5G telephone poles in England to stop the Chinese from sending the virus through radio waves.

Through a tiny square on my screen, I watch one classmate shoo her puppy away and another shoo away his mom, who was wondering if he wants steak or chicken for dinner. An analyst's child toddles into the frame and tugs on his shirt. He sits her down in front of the TV—Peppa Pig. Dogs and mothers and toddlers simply don't get that we are in class, discussing very very important things.

Tasked with writing my own stories, I cold email dozens of experts, asking if they can spare a minute to talk to a college student about the effects of this virus on their respective areas of expertise.

I sign each message,

> Hope you and your loved ones are staying sane
> and healthy in these unprecedented times!"
> All the best,
> Owen Matthews

Then I go for a run. Another trip through pandemic-spawned paradise.

Story by
RT Lundquist

The One Without Judgment

Sometimes it's not your fault if you're broken.

I've learned this lesson a number of different ways, over a number of years.

The cracks took some time to get used to, but I managed.

Sad to say, I have come to realize that the very reason for my existence is rather averse to flaws.

I have a major one.

Because of this, they say all manner of things:

"Oh, seven years of bad luck!"

"How am I supposed to see clearly?"

"It should be replaced!"

And I have yet to be replaced. It could be that I am loved, which is unlikely. It is more likely that I am without excess cost, and therefore irreplaceable for the time being.

I'll take it, really. I have come to love my job, though they say awful things to my face.

My job is a glimpse into people's lives, and I see the beauty that comes out when they think no one is looking.

Or the madness, which is also a gift to me. It provides a sense of empathy that hadn't yet made itself known in my mind.

My job is a chance to show them their true colors and help them change for the better.

I see when they are hurt, and though they can't bear to meet my gaze, I am there in case they need me, to remind them of who they are.

I see when they are joyous and rejoice with them, matching their joviality with my own and encouraging them in their way.

I see when they need to recall their own beauty, which is almost never necessary.

And though it hurts, at times I show them something they don't want to see.

That is how I came to be broken, I think. Too many disappointments from one hurt person.

I forgave them; for after it happened, I understood.

I saw the same disgust on different faces. I saw the same rejection.

Yet I stayed.

I did my job as best I could, despite my brokenness.

I still do.

I still see people walk in, start to have a conversation with me—more a visual one than a verbal, it must be said—then stop and frown at my flaws, and leave without another word or glance.

I try to ignore them and give them the benefit of the doubt.

Maybe they, in all of their perfection, had never seen a broken thing before.

It wasn't my fault, but maybe they didn't realize that.

If they couldn't blame me, I wouldn't blame them.

I work all day every day as I do, and get some rest in between. There are good, rare times when I meet a person who I really love from the start. That person will walk in, remind themselves of who they are, and once more turn to go. Before they leave, however, they'll look at me and say with an air of finality that gives me hope,

"A cracked mirror means *good* luck if I want it to."

Then they toss their hair and stride out the door.

Giving a Mongoose a Plastic Bottle

In my motherland, I see

a mongoose sinking

its warrior teeth into plastic trash.

The sunlight reflects its struggle,

plastic across the oceans, across

rice fields, across a cardboard

building where a forest

once breathed. This land

gave me a life & I've

given it bottle caps. Warning:

Choking Hazard—mongoose

can't read. Immune to snake

venom, susceptible to plastic

bottles. The lake has closed

its eyes—closed its eyes &

swallowed brown water, sprinkled

with plastic bags. Warning:

To avoid danger of suffocation,

keep this plastic bag away

from babies & children (& lakes

& oceans & mongooses

& hornbills & turtles &

peacocks & rice fields

& forests & deserts &

& & &)

Holding the Village Ashes

for the Rohingya people

Summer came & left on the same
scorched foot, covered in village
ashes & coughing fits. What is left
are a million minds, filled
with empty roofs & broken glass.
One million souls with just one
wish—too much, they say,
as the boat quietly drowns.
They use the oars to spoon salt
water, one more tongue to barely
keep alive. Money on walls,
money on drones, money not on
the village ashes. In the camp,
a child colors a picture—houses
on fire: red, orange, gold, blue—
all the colors that ashes are not.
When the monsoon falls over
the settled village ashes, the land
drinks & it drinks & it sinks
without feet.

Ghazal for All the World

What will become of a burning world
when ice melts her feet on this burning world?

The Himalaya mountains smile in pain:
they know the taste of a churning world.

A breeze morphs, whisks away his son,
before he jolts on this turning world.

An apple that rolls at the base of a tree
is tossed far beyond this learning world.

Here, a parade for a shining girl,
there, a star and a yearning world.

A galaxy dissolves its own withering face:
lost is the bliss of this returning world.

border violence

this is where   i draw a line

   i say   to the words

that tear me apart   in two

   & now i will tell you   there

are words in my fists

   that are carefully hand-picked

correctly spelled because these

   are not true mistakes

just fables   of mankind

it is not the words   it is

the people   who laugh

  at splitting bodies from afar

those are the people it is them

  whom i ask   who *are* you

from where   have you built

  your arrogance   is it fenced

is it concrete   does it split me

  vertically   or horizontally

Elegy on June 24

*for Oscar and Valeria Martínez, who drowned while crossing
the Mexican border*

A precious ladybug,

red pants & black shoes—

this delicate girl

with her wings sweeping

over her father's back.

Bodies floating

& terror sinking,

just a month short

of two & a breath short

of peace.

The earth watches

the floating clouds, one

with the summer sun.

Desert sands come

bringing the news,

as the noise

lightly dies away.

The border slowly

swims away, drowning

in its own sin.

Monday's Coastal Report

has arrived: reeds, fear,

empty beer bottles,

water-logged hope,

two immigrants face down

praying for peace.

After Kendrick Lamar

Promise that you will sing about me,

Promise that you will sing about me.

I heard that all black boys are doomed to die by bullets,

Bound to have their blood spilled onto pavement

Before becoming graduates,

I heard that all black boys are born

To have their faces sprawled across a white tee,

You see, I hear so many black boys are offered

County or casket, with no hope for college,

I heard black bodies are good at catching casings.

Black blood must be magnetic.

Must yearn for a shell casing's kiss,

Must feel like home,

I heard that bullets love to explore brown body cavities,

That excavation is a bullet's favorite hobby,

Heard that melanin must be polarized

The way that even saying their names

Can rip a country in half.

Promise me when the lights shut off

And it's my turn, to settle down, my main concern,

I heard all black boys are doomed to die by bullets

But before my number is called

Promise that you will sing about me,

Promise that you will sing about me.

The Cost of Existence

When you're born, flesh bathed in mahogany,

In the land, where your kind stay in season,

After season, after season, after season,

You know the root of all evil dwells in the neighborhoods

You never look like you belong in.

Where melanin stay mistaken for malevolence

And assumption delineates identity.

When you're born, skin akin to obsidian,

In the land, where your mere existence is resistance,

And it doesn't matter if there's a witness,

You know to be self-aware,

Less you dare offend Massa officer,

Else his bad day, be your doomsday,

The fast lane on the highway, to oblivion.

When you're born swaddled in a topaz facade,

In a land bathed in the blood of kin,

You know existence between

The White Man's Burden and a sunken place,

A space, where the good air don't reach yo neighborhood,

Where hoods, remind you the air is saturated with hate,

And whispers from audacious allies,

Come gift wrapped in sweet nothings.

Rage

What do you know about rage, about fury,

About being entombed by your deepest frustrations

As your nation, makes up excuses for public executions,

Call him a criminal, that's just 5-0 subliminal for n****r.

Feel bigger? Feel like a man for murder in the -th degree,

Your pedigree ought to be proud.

And I'm not talking about Uncle Sam,

The Cracka that never gave a damn who the hell I am,

Nor what I stand, kneel, march,

Scream and write this poem for, simply finds it a chore

To see us as anything more than fodder

Or filling for body bags, and white folk dare to even ask,

Well, what about black-on-black crime, every single time

And the "allies" are no better.

Wielding allyship as an "I'm not racist" prize

Cause you just now realize

My people are practically lambs for the slaughter,

Raising our sons and daughters in a perpetual state of fear.

But let me be clear, this here is a hurt you will ever know.

We don't show on the daily, how insanely furious we truly are.

You never see the rage, the fury.

And nah we don't trust no jury

Of the just-us system, Like, you wanted justice?

Sorry, you just missed him, just went on paid vacation.

He's already left the station,

But if you just be patient, he'll be back.

And we've been waiting justice for generations.

So, when it comes to these situations,

Where we take out our frustrations, in cities across the nation,

I say to hell with appropriation, to hell with respectability

The question is are you hearing me

Instead of merely fearing me?

Trust that I've got more fear in me,

Than the entirety of your ancestry.

So, tell me, what do you know about rage,

About a Facebook page littered with lynchings?

Which brings me to the question of the day,

How many times have you seen yourself murdered today??

Sins of the Father

An Epiphany Only a Dream Could Deliver

The marrow of my bones was surely drained—injected with liquid cement—because each step takes all of my strength. My twin sister, Hailey, drags slowly behind me, stumbling and tripping over the lips of the craters that my feet imprint in the marble tile. The hold I have on her bony wrist fails to waver. We move together. We must move forward together. Once we reach the end of the grand room, we're confronted by an imposing dark oak desk. I break a vertebra in my neck in order to view the stork nesting behind it.

The stork wears an orange waistcoat; the thin golden chain of a pocket watch dangles elegantly out of the coat's breast pocket. He lowers his bill to gaze out over his clear teashades at us. The loud tick of the stork's watch is like a drumbeat in my ear. He extends a wing out before us. With little hesitation Hailey offers him her tiny hand, and the space between the stork and us shortens drastically as he flips her hand around and around and around.

The stork tsks when he glides the black tip of his wing through the divots between her fingers. "My, my . . ." the stork whispers to himself, fascinated.

He gently drops her hand, then reaches for mine.

I inhale, then surrender my hand to the large bird, holding my breath as I do so. His beady, coal-like eyes quadruple in size as he studies the back of my hand, then my palm. His throat clicks. "Oh no," he squawks.

I flinch when he begins to trace the lines of my palm with his wing tip. "Bad is what you are." I squirm and fight as he pulls me roughly against his feathered chest. "You're badly broken and broken badly. *Bad! Bad! Bad!*" He punctuates each word with a wing flap on the back.

The stork shoves me off his chest. My sister becomes smaller and smaller as I plunge downward, deep into the flames dancing between the cracked marble.

Spitting Image / Metamorphosis

Though it becomes harder to deny the truth the older I become, I try not to notice it. Really, I do. Besides, it's close to impossible to avoid mirrors and reflective surfaces (*all* of the time). But I try.

I try not to notice how much I look like my father.

When I entered my teenage years, family members couldn't resist cooing about how much of a "little Sean-y Mike" I was turning into. Not wanting to fight my grandmother, or great-aunts and -uncles, I would offer tight-lipped smiles and stiff shrugs. I didn't want to believe them, and I didn't at first.

I don't recall how or why the fight began, but it came to an abrupt end when I raised my voice at her. Hailey sat cross-legged on the stool in front of her vanity. She looked at me through the slim left-side mirror, the bristles of the makeup brush ceased their forward trajectory midway to her turned cheek.

"What?" I snapped.

I noticed how her eyes were becoming glossy in the mirror, so I stared at my reflection, not wanting to see her cry.

My cheeks were flushed, dusted red by anger.

My pupils were tight, pinpricks of black.

I couldn't blink away my father's face, so I turned my back to the mirror and walked out of the room, praying she didn't see what I did.

The Rot of a Tree Goes Only as Far as Its Roots (A-Side)

My greatest fear in life is to become my father.

I cup my hands under the faucet, filling them with water to splash against the porcelain. I watch as strands of dark blond hair swirl around the rusted drain until ultimately committing suicide. My hairline is receding at the temples; the texture of my hair is thinning. I'm balding.

My greatest fear in life is to become my father.

It was nearly midnight when the shrill ring of the landline startled my grandfather, my father's stepdad, awake. Exhausted from truck driving for two days without more than an eight-hour break, my grandfather fell asleep in the recliner while watching the late-night news. He lifted the cold dinner tray from his lap and set it on the coffee table to walk into the dark kitchen to answer the phone.

"Hello?" my grandfather groaned into the receiver, rubbing the sleep from his eyes with his free hand.

"Is Sean there?" the man on the other end replied.

My grandfather sighed. Of course a call this late at night would be Sean-related.

"No. He's at a friend's house."

It was a Friday night, the kickoff to a weekend full of drug- and alcohol-fueled partying for my father before his final week of high school. "Well, when you see him, tell him I'm gonna pound his f---ing face in!"

The line went dead.

My grandfather put the phone back on the hook. "Dumbass didn't even leave his name," he said into the night as he clicked off the TV, then walked down the hall to join his wife in bed.

A few days later, my grandfather overheard my father brag to his buddies about how he "beat Nick to the honeymoon." My grandfather knew Nick—he was a close friend of Sean's. After all the neighborhood boys left for their own homes, my grandfather questioned my father about what he meant. My father had slept with Nick's fiancé at some spring break party.

She and Nick were supposed to marry after graduation. Sean was supposed to be in their wedding. My grandfather was dumbfounded. "Why?"

My father shrugged. "Because I could."

The landline rang; a week had passed since their talk. It was another friend of Sean's. My grandfather passed my father the phone. The call was over in minutes. Sean hung up, then walked calmly into his room and shut the door behind him.

The following day in the obituary section of the Sunday paper, my grandfather read that Nick had died. He later learned that the young man had hung himself in the basement of his parents' home.

My greatest fear in life is to become my father.

You Slitgut Sonavabitch!

The small village of Hilliards, Pennsylvania, could always tell when my great-grandfather was drinking. It's not like his neighbors were nosy. They didn't peer over the windowsill that gave sight into the living room of the Woolcutt home; they weren't gossips. They wouldn't be able to hear themselves even if they were, over whatever Johnny Cash song Great-Grandfather Ken chose to blare that particular night. They wouldn't even be able to see my great-grandfather, likely slumped over drunk on the greasy recliner chair (or beating on Great-Grandma with one hand while holding a can of beer in the other), due to the speaker that was perched on the windowsill.

My father once told me Great-Grandpa Ken was the best man I will never have the privilege of meeting—told me Grandpa Ken was the closest thing to a father he had.

The Rot of a Tree Goes Only as Far as Its Roots (B-Side)

My greatest fear in life is to become my father.

I listen to fast, angry music with growling vocals and heavy guitar. I enjoy bands like Deftones, A Perfect Circle, and Black Flag. I burned through three sets of earbuds in two months after my mom died because I couldn't go to sleep without them plugged in my ears at full volume.

My greatest fear in life is to become my father.

Krystal's eyes stung, stung so badly that if they weren't watering every time she blinked, she'd probably cry—cry hard like the twin babies squirming in the playpen at her feet. The twins had been released from the NICU and cleared to return home the day before. They seemed so *peaceful* swaddled in their incubators, but that peace was lost once they arrived home. Cried, that's all they did. Both babies turned away from warm bottles; kicked and twisted as they were rocked; screamed when they were cooed at—no matter what Krystal did, she couldn't seem to soothe her restless children.

But Krystal was *tired*; her feet were swollen from constantly being on them the past two days; all she wanted was to sit down and *sleep*. So she did. She plopped down on the living room couch and slipped into the darkness behind her eyes.

Immense heat spread rapidly from the crook of her inner elbow to the rest of her body. Krystal was on *fire*—her skin engulfed in flames. Her eyes ripped open and moved to her right side. Sean was there, kneeling beside the couch's armrest, syringe held between his pointer and middle finger, in the same manner one holds a cigarette.

"What are you doing?" she screeched.

Sean untied the rubber tube from around her arm. "Nothin'," he replied as he wrapped the tube around his own arm. "Just helping you relax."

Nausea unfurled in her stomach. Krystal thought she was going to be sick.

My greatest fear in life is to become my father.

I have a short temper and am quick to frustrate—to yell, to allow blistering rage to travel up my chest, my neck, then finally seep and spread under the flesh covering my skull.

My greatest fear in life is to become my father, to age like my great-grandfather, and to die like my biological grandfather—to nurture the rot plaguing the roots of my Family Tree. I want to be good. And sometimes I start to believe that I am good, but then I catch sight of my reflection while walking past the bathroom mirror or see my framed picture on the wall and remember who I am and what twisted tree I fell from.

I anticipate the day I wake up and look over my shoulder to see that I've shed my skin, [name]'s skin, during the night. I wait for my piercings, scars, moles, and bruises to lay in a terribly wrinkled heap on my mattress. I wait until I am rendered bald and lose the shine in my eyes. I wait to look in the mirror only to see my father staring back at me.

But until I finally become my father, I'll try to be good.

Basically just good.

A Minor Inheritance

14

A week into quarantine, I found an English-Tagalog dictionary.

Twenty-one years in the same house, and I'd never seen it before. It was nestled among James Patterson thrillers and Nora Roberts romances, in a bin that had been packed away in the shed last fall when I'd moved into my first apartment.

I sat down on my bedroom floor, surrounded by books I'd already pulled out and a week's worth of laundry that I needed to put away. The dictionary's once crimson cover had faded to a pinky-red. Oddly enough, the yellow title reminded me of the walls of my older brother's childhood room, inspired by his favorite Disney movie: a warm, soft gold, shades away from the color of Sheriff Woody's shirt.

I opened to the first page. A third edition, copyrighted 1992 by the Commission on the Filipino Language, originally published in 1960 by the Institute of National Language. A second printing of the first edition took place in 1974, only a year after my father, uncle, and grandparents immigrated to the United States.

Apparently the original Filipino alphabet had only fourteen letters. Certain consonants weren't used, and vowels were simplified to three symbols. Then the Spanish colonized the Philippines, and the cultures began to intertwine. It became necessary to incorporate more letters—the alphabet fluctuating between twenty-eight and thirty-two characters— as communication developed and names were adopted and created through the blending of bloodlines.

I really wonder if those added letters allowed Filipinos to say more. If there were certain words in Spanish that didn't translate well into Tagalog but captured a feeling, an action that had been unexpressed or unacknowledged until then. Or if those letters just complicated things. Brought in more frustration, more uncertainty, and more silence as language and identities transformed.

I struggle enough trying to express myself with English's twenty-six letters. If more letters were suddenly added to the alphabet, even just one more, would I be able to say more? Could I? Would it be easier to talk to my dad without casting seeds of guilt with one careless word?

I wandered out into the living room, the sound of my footsteps bouncing between the darkly streaked bamboo flooring and knotty pine ceiling. Dad was watching *The Last Samurai* now that Mom had crawled into bed and couldn't sigh her way through the action scenes. I sat on the couch next to him, the leather squeaking as I cuddled into his side. I knew that Tom Cruise was short, but the traditional armor seemed to sit heavily on his frame, making him even shorter.

Without turning to look at Dad, I asked, "Does Uncle Ed know more Filipino dishes? I mean besides adobo and pansit?" These, fried rice, and lumpia (egg rolls) were the only Filipino foods that my family had made as I grew up. I have a vague recollection of my grandparents visiting when I was maybe 8 years old. My grandma wasn't yet having trouble with her heart and memory or exhausting herself trying to take care of my demanding and stroke-weakened grandfather. She still gardened and cooked. She'd made some kind of fish resting on a bed of bright, sautéed bell peppers, with the scales, head, and tail still on. I ate a lot of rice that night.

Dad paused the movie and cocked his head at me; the low light from the wall sconces flashed and glared off his glasses. "Yeah, he does. Why?"

I tucked the blanket tighter around my feet. They always got so cold at home, no matter what. "I just want to try connecting more with Filipino culture, I guess."

"Well, there's, like, Filipino clubs and things in the cities, if you wanted to—"

"No, Dad. I don't think I would be ready to do that. I'm familiar with food . . . comfortable with it. I think it might be a good way to start. Something small." I tried to give him a reassuring smile. "Besides, it'd be nice to cook with Uncle Ed. Especially now that I can legally drink."

He smiled back, the dimple in his left cheek winking. I had gotten my smile from him, but not the dimple. "I'm sure he'd like that. Yeah, Uncle Ed probably remembers more than I do about things. I mean, I was pretty young when we came over."

"Eleven and 9, I remember." I did. I'd been only 7, and my older brother, Drew, had been almost 9 when Dad took his naturalization test.

"It's not as though I meant to keep these things from you, Anna. I had to try and fit in, be American and all that." Dad twisted, turned to face me more directly.

"I know, Dad." I did. I remember his stories about growing up in New Hope, Minnesota. Two Asian boys speaking formal, proper English in a neighborhood full of African Americans. Target practice. Uncle Eddy doing his best to protect Dad and himself from bullies. Almost fifty years later, I knew that it still happened to incoming immigrants.

I took a deep breath. "I know—" *I did*. "—that you didn't really have a choice. But it doesn't really feel like I have one either."

Dad was quiet. My dark hair slid from behind my ear. Another thing that I had gotten from him, although now his was littered with gray and seriously thinning. I looked at the TV. We had let it sit too long. Netflix was running through its slideshow of new series and movies. There was another season of some show called *3%*. Two crumbling cliffs separated by water—each with a pair of characters staring stoically across at the other—lit up the screen before fading out into women with huge hair and sparkly leotards in various fighting positions.

"I mean, people see me, and they make these assumptions. I feel like I've experienced what it's like to be Filipino on the outside. I got more money from St. Thomas because of it.

People have been racist toward me. But I don't *feel* Filipino on the inside. There's no connection. And that's not your fault, you know?" Did he? Dad wouldn't really look at me. I wrapped my arm around his shoulders, snuggling close to his side. "I just want to be able to learn and see and decide for myself.

Namesake

When Drew was born, my parents named him after Dad's best friend, Andrew, and Dad's older brother, Edward. A year and a half later, they took a similar approach with me. I'm named after the two women whom my mother loved most: her late French-Canadian grandmother, Anna, and her older sister, Lisa.

Traditionally, Filipino children's middle names are the mother's maiden name. Example:

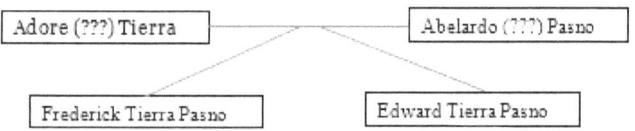

Grandma had been upset, to put it mildly. Aunt Lisa was flattered, but also argued that I should have a different middle name: Elsie, after their Swedish grandmother. That way, I would be named for both of my great-grandmothers on Mom's side.

Drew and I weren't through disappointing. After each of us was born and visitors were allowed, Aunt Lisa took one look at us—tiny, wrinkled, red—and said: *Where's my brown baby?*

Hyphen

On the way to Dad's naturalization test, I sat in the back row of our Honda Odyssey, chomping on the striped pillow mints given to me by my first-grade teacher.

I was bragging about how I got to explain to my class that my daddy had to take a special test. Drew was more interested in seeing if the sucker he was gnawing at had gum in the middle. He'd had Mrs. Johnson last year, so she'd given me a goodie bag for him too. Mom and Aunt Lisa nodded and oohed and ahhed like they were watching fireworks.

I nodded eagerly at the attention; chest puffed, I spun the miniature U.S. flag in between my sticky palms. "Yeah, I'm pretty special. I'm the only little black girl in my class!"

Mom and Aunt Lisa laughed. Dad chuckled from behind the wheel, his eyes meeting mine in the rearview mirror. I clenched my hand tight around the flag's plastic stick. Aunt Lisa wiped tears from her eyes, tried to catch her breath, and I chomped on another mint, wrinkled the happy wrapper that I had stripped off of the candy.

They explained: I—and Dad and Drew—were Filipino-American. Pacific Islanders. (Although now I think I'm supposed to check Asian on official forms, surveys, and free trial accounts?) Not black.

This is the first time that I distinctly remember being told how I was supposed to identify. Maybe my parents had told me before. Maybe not enough.

Maybe I had learned about different races in school. How much racial history do first-graders learn now? Or maybe I had just absorbed in binary: black and white. I knew about Native Americans and connected them to pilgrims and Thanksgiving.

I had seen Disney's *Pocahontas*, was amazed at the way she stood up to her father even though she was a daddy's girl like me. But as far as I knew, she wasn't a real person, just a cartoon. She'd saved her tribe but had to lose John Smith all the same. I was always sad that they didn't end up together, like other Disney princess movies. Not quite a happy ending. But maybe happy enough because the film—and the sequel—didn't even begin to cover the making and breaching of unfair treaties, reduction of tribal lands, massacres, and boarding schools aimed to erase Native American peoples.

But we'd talked about presidents: all those important, dead white men. Like Abraham Lincoln. And how important he was to ending slavery for black people. I think we spent more time on that than Native Americans.

And so, my mind clung to sightings of the handful of actually black students that "diversified" my elementary school, to the history I had learned about people who I didn't exactly look like, but resembled more closely than any of my white classmates, teachers, and family.

I didn't talk much for the rest of the car ride. Instead, I picked at the cheap, waxy pencils Mrs. Johnson had put in my goodie bag. As soon as I sharpened them, the design would peel off in thin strips, revealing the plain white surface underneath.

Homecoming

Was it two or three days after my grandpa died, as I was sitting down to dinner with family friends in my childhood home, that I saw the Philippines through my grandma's eyes?

Just before he died, Dad and Mom, Aunt Lisa, and a couple family friends flew out to Florida to try to settle my grandparents' estate. No one from our family had visited and seen the state of the house in at least seven years. (It had been hard enough to organize trips when we were children, and now that all of us grandchildren were officially in our 20s, occupied with college and jobs, it was next to impossible.) My parents thought it would be okay. My Aunt Lyn and Uncle Ed were staying with Grandma at our house. Grandpa was doing . . . okay in the nursing home.

My parents were there for less than twenty-four hours and had begun interviewing potential estate sale companies and realtors, and organizing the house when they received the call. Aunt Lisa and one friend stayed to keep working. Faced with the threat of an early April blizzard, everyone else hopped on the very next flight back to Minnesota.

The day after they got home (so it must've been two days after Grandpa had died), my parents picked me up from college; I was in a sleep-deprived daze. There was only a month of spring semester left, and I had to bring every textbook home. When we got out of the car, Dad didn't even tease that the weight of my bag was going to break my back or, worse, his. Our house seemed full of Grandma's sadness and the responsibilities that avalanched my parents.

That night, Anne—the other friend who'd gone to Florida—swept into our house like Mary Poppins. My parents had met her at our church years ago. Anne had twelve siblings and four kids of her own, the last of whom was just finishing high school. Many of her siblings had their own businesses and families and were more than happy to help each other out, no questions asked; they attended Mass and volunteered at church regularly. Their roots and history were embedded in the town's foundation.

She'd rung our doorbell, her husband hovering behind her, and placed a sheet tray with a large salmon filet covered in lemon wheels in Dad's hands.

"I'm making you dinner, Freddy," she declared. With tasteful pink lip gloss and a thick cap of near-white blond hair shining, Anne strode into the house and hugged my grandma.

Grandma loved Anne. She thought Anne was funny and had wonderful taste—claims that I stand by—but mostly, I think Grandma loved Anne because she always listened whenever Grandma talked.

Throughout their marriage, Grandpa would continually interrupt or scold Grandma if he thought she talked too much. Later, when his multiple strokes and diabetes rendered him unable to take care of himself, he would yell and criticize.

That night at dinner, almost sixty years' worth of unfinished or repressed stories seemed to spill out:

Once, when Uncle Ed was little, he took two eggs from a bowl on a table and cracked them against each other. When the bright yolks and fractured shells slipped to the floor, he giggled and said, "*Oh, what a waste!*" before doing it again and again and again. So naughty. I grinned. Uncle Ed still loved to cause trouble.

Of course, that would've never happened when Grandma was growing up with her six siblings; her mother arranged the dinner table so a younger child was always between two older children. In this every-other system, the older siblings would make sure the little ones behaved: sitting nicely, eating politely, not speaking unless spoken to. As one of the oldest, Grandma did this throughout her childhood.

She and her sisters all went to the same school. After they had all gotten married, some of her nieces and nephews went there too. Here, Grandma pulled out a picture. (There were many more that Mom had ripped out of photo albums and shoved into a box during the brief Florida trip.)

I stared at the faded image for a moment. Grandma and her sisters are smiling with their hair styled and clothes pressed. They're standing in a single line in front of a school, a little girl (probably a niece) in a tidy uniform tucked in front of them, just to the left of center. Grandma might be in her thirties here. I'd only seen one photo of her as a young woman before—a formal portrait—taken when she was about 24. At 20, I wondered how closely I resembled her: dark hair pulled back, a long forehead, large dark eyes, a wide nose, and full lips.

Now 86, she ran both hands through her short hair, thin and brittle from being overtreated with Revlon's Light Golden-Brown hair dye. I stared at her nails, carefully clipped and shaped from the manicure I'd given her earlier that day; she had already begun to chip off the white gold polish.

Grandma's family was luckier than most. Their father owned a pharmacy, which many of them worked at as they grew older. Leftover from eras of colonization—first by the Spanish and then the Americans—the wealth and opportunities were mostly reserved for the elite. So many relied on the land and agriculture to support themselves. Nearly fifty years after my grandparents left to escape the Marcos dictatorship, the government corruption and economic disparity is no less alarming.

Grandpa's family had owned so much land and many businesses in the Philippines. That's why they had to leave. Apparently, Marcos was limiting the amount of land a person could hold—at least for people who weren't in his back pocket.

I blew out a long breath and took another bite of the fish that Anne had made. The fact that we'd had plantations and Marcos's corrupt land redistribution policies, I'd known about. I was doing a series of papers and presentations about the People Power Movement's overthrow of Marcos for a class on active nonviolence. I'd been horrified at the possibility that my family could've been one of the economic elites that had supported and perpetuated the dictatorship.

But no. They'd left, and everything was split between Grandpa's four brothers. (Aunt Lyn and Uncle Ed were to deal with whatever property was left to inherit, because Mom and Dad were handling all the paperwork in the States.)

But Grandpa was so smart. According to Grandma, Grandpa had come up with a new way to dry out coconuts on their plantations. They sat on raised platforms so they were more exposed to the air.

Grandma paused, played with the heavy gold and diamond rings on arthritis-swollen knuckles and then Grandpa's pendant; she fussed with how the large rectangle of brilliant jade, framed in rich yellow-gold, lay on her gray crew neck, its hems stained and frayed. Probably some old sweat shirt that she had kept from Dad and Uncle Ed's high school years. Although Grandma usually liked to dress up for company, she hadn't disappeared into our basement-turned-apartment to change when Ann had arrived.

She folded her hands on the table and closed her eyes, face tilted up to the warm but artificial light from our dining room chandelier. Maybe she'd done this countless times in the Philippines: head tipped back, squinting at the ever-shifting sunlight that filtered through the palm fronds; her sons chased each other beneath the trees, laughing and winding between trunks that had grown tall and strong through generations of Pasnoes. Dad and Uncle Ed had probably whined for pineapple or sugar cane to gnaw on, too impatient to wait for lunch or dinner. What had it been like to be embraced by that rich tropical air? What was it like for her now, her 4-foot, 10-inch frame stripped of warmth by the Midwest's early spring wind the minute she stepped outside?

She wanted to go back. Back to the Philippines, back to their grand white house near the coast or the lavish penthouse apartment over a shop they rented in the city; back to one of her few remaining sisters, Yoli, whose children Grandma insisted would take care of them both; back to see the places where she had grown up and studied and fell in love and given birth to her sons. She wanted to die there.

Maybe she thought that such a homecoming would replace what she saw as the tattered remains of her life here.

Headliner

"Okay," I glanced up at Ms. Spoerl. "Ready?"

The speech coach, musical and play director, NHS advisor, and my personal role model nodded. "Ready." She perched on the edge of her front table. I sat opposite from her on the tall stool she taught from occasionally; the dull yellow leather of the seat creaked as I shifted to open my notebook.

I pressed Record on my phone. Spoerl also taught English 9, Honors English 10, AP Language and Composition, but unfortunately *not* the only creative writing class that Somerset High School offered. With a little over 500 kids and less than ideal funding, teachers were spread pretty thin; if she had taught it instead of Mrs. Kadlec, maybe I could've convinced her that *creative writing* was more along the lines of short stories, imagery exercises, poems, comics—*anything* but oral histories.

I sighed, rolled my shoulders back, and tried to keep most of the exasperation out of my voice as I began to interview Spoerl about her experience directing *Bye Bye Birdie* last fall. This creative writing elective was the one fun class I'd allowed myself senior year in a schedule packed with pre-calc, Spanish 4, music, and AP classes—anything and everything to increase potential scholarships. I scribbled the titles of other potential musicals that Spoerl rattled off that she and the choir director had considered before deciding on *Bye Bye Birdie*.

"So how did you decide on who to cast for the leads?" I smiled a little. I had played the main female lead, sassy Rose Alvarez, and killed it. Maybe a compliment or two would make this project more bearable.

"Well, I mean a lot of the upper classmen were really solid. Cade, Nikki, Janae, Ethan, and Mitch were all in show choir and speech, so they had a lot of experience with choreography and performing." Spoerl leaned back on her desk, legs crossed at the ankles. She was wearing her bubble-gum pink heels today, my favorite out of her many pairs. "But there was some debate over why you were cast as Rosie."

I pulled my attention from Spoerl's shoes. The line of audio on my voice memo app, which had been spiking and fluctuating to capture each nuance of sound, flatlined.

"What do you mean by that exactly?"

Spoerl sighed. She uncrossed her ankles, sat a little straighter, and crossed them again. She brushed a wave of short, dark blond hair behind her ear. "I didn't tell you this at the time because I'd wanted you to focus and enjoy the role—" *Well DUH.* "—but some people questioned if we cast you as Rosie . . . because you could pass as Latina."

The week after the final performance, my Algebra II teacher had taken a moment to congratulate everyone who'd been involved in the musical. He'd gone to see it with his 7-year-old daughter. He told me that she'd asked him if the main girl (me) was Spanish.

I'd laughed, said no, that I'd just been taking Spanish for three years at the high school. "Nope, not Spanish. I'm actually half Filipino."

He apologized. I smiled and waved away his apology. I had been kind of flattered that I'd been so convincing. "It's okay."

I clutched at the leather stool now, trying to anchor myself. *No.* My notebook slid off my lap. *No. It's not okay.*

Spoerl was staring at me. I licked my chapped lips, scoffed; my breathing was quick, and my necklace felt hot and strangling. "Are you kidding me?" I jumped off the stool. Although my feet had only been maybe 6 inches off the ground, the impact jarred me. I paced. I looked at Spoerl for answers, for denial. Powerless, her face was pinched and concerned, hands limp in her lap.

I turned sharply on my heel, ponytail stinging across my face. A laugh escaped, harsh and ragged. "You've got to be joking. Seriously? I've been in choir since freshman year, just like everyone else. I'm in speech too! I competed at State last year!"

"Exactly." Ms. Spoerl stood, placed a hand on my shoulder. "And you prepared for the audition. You worked for that part. That's why we picked you."

I couldn't stop. "Yeah, I did work for it! I was sick when I sang and auditioned, and I was still better than anyone else! People honestly think that I got it just because of how I looked? What, should I have covered myself in white paint for my call back? Or maybe for a performance? Would that have proved that I got to play Rosie because I deserved it?"

I felt like crying. Throwing a tantrum. Ripping out the shitty notes I'd taken for a project I didn't care about. I wanted to broadcast the interview across the PA system and interrogate just who thought my appearance was worth more than my talent.

I'm certain that I did none of those things. Most likely, I picked up my notebook and sat back down on the tall yellow stool. I might've tossed my hair back, blown out a long sigh, muttered under my breath, but read the next question on my list. I had an assignment to complete after all. I wasn't about to let my feelings get in the way of my GPA.

The interview was lost when I upgraded phones. Rereading that oral history report, I didn't find any mention that people had assumed I'd been typecast. I don't remember if Spoerl answered the questions I had shouted at her. Even now, I can't imagine anything she could've said.

Nearly a senior in college, set to graduate and attempt to be an adult, I experienced this incident almost four years ago. I see more similarities between Rosie and me than I did then. Mae—Rose's fiancé's white, racist, and overbearing mother—never thought Rose was good enough for her son, Albert, because she was Latina. It didn't matter how loyal she'd been to the failing record company he had inherited. Her physical appearance (and the language, culture, and traditions associated with it) was enough to discredit her other traits and abilities.

I hadn't thought about my Maes. Hadn't considered that they could possibly exist in a town where I had lived all my life. I didn't know that anybody even saw just how many shades darker my skin was. That it apparently erased everything else about me.

Even if I had been able to swallow the burning tightness of hurt, shame, and frustration that constricted my rib cage like a corset, how could I have defended myself against comments I'd been happily, ignorantly blind and deaf to because I hadn't seen myself as different. And I *still* couldn't see or hear them, couldn't pinpoint the origin, point a finger and say "AHA! So *you're* the culprit! *You're* my Mae. *You're* the racist." Besides Spoerl's words, I had no evidence, no proof, no personal, physical experience of racism besides the heavy, ugly rattling in my chest.

But Rose was able to spit back clever responses to Mae, find closure and triumph over her snide bias. She took all of those things that Mae attacked her for, exaggerated them until Mae was the one who was frustrated and uncomfortable— became "Spanish Rose."

"Spanish Rose" had been my favorite number; it took place after Rose walked out on Albert (and his mother) and immediately attempted to start her love life anew in a local bar. I had found the perfect dress: flapper-esque, with rows upon rows of red fringe that perfectly matched my lipstick and hat. In the number's opening chords, I pouted on a barstool and growled out the first lyrics—another refrain to the endless microaggression "But where are you *really* from?"

The pit band paused so I could strike a pose and playfully slip into a thick Spanish accent, cultivated over three intense years of Spanish class with Señora Turner. My rolled r's had been high and trilling, vibrating notes all their own to set the flirty, sassy tone for the solo. The spotlight tracked me across the stage and cast everything but slivers of background into obscurity. My brown skin, wide nose, dark eyes and hair—all shining under the lights and on display for my mostly white school. I had looked different, and now I was finally acting different too; every twist of my hips, every hair toss, every twirling hand cemented the fact that I could pass as *Spanish Ana.*

When I think of how I would perform now, everything rings with fury and the *fuck you* that should've been there all along:

All right. Sure. Spanish. [A snarl in place of a smirk on red lips.] As Spanish as you can take! [Glare up at the blinding spot forced to follow me across the stage.]

Pendejo, let me give you a little advice. [Crook a finger and saunter closer to the audience. Don't heed the mantra of all theater departments: More blush, or you'll be washed out! Anger and disgust provide color enough.]

To cross Spanish Ana—not wise. Don't make a sound, don't mess around. [The flush and heat crawl up, burn my ears amid the tight curls and pins that dig into my scalp, all tucked beneath a carefully positioned hat.]

Her heart is as cold as ice! [Would they understand? Would they know it was their fault? Would they be grateful that the dark could hide their own identities and judgments?]

Well, now you've met Spanish Ana . . . [Hat still swept off my head here. Exaggerate a bow because clearly, they hadn't known me before.] *You'll NEVER forget her now!* [The hat flung into the audience this time, not tossed into a shadowed corner of the stage, hastily collected and tucked away in the dark before the next scene.]

[No, the lights begin to come up over the audience. No more hiding. An accusing finger jabs at the sea of white.]

Not German . . . And not French . . . Or Swedish . . . Or Irish . . . But Spaaaaaaaaaaaaaaaaaaaaa— [a long, slow sweep of a hand across my brown skin; a reminder that they chose to see me this way. Not as an actress, a musician, a bookworm, an artist, a 4.0 student, an overthinker, a writer, a friend, a person, but some goddamn fucking stereotype.] *—nish Ana!*

[Flip middle fingers with a flourish. Lights come down. End scene.]

It would begin with women caressing my hair,

with the hand of my mother.

Every man I've ever laid with exists purely to serve chilled
wine at 5 o'clock.

My body would be sculpted out of velvet and my eyes nothing
but glazed marble.

There, every hip I touch would turn to gold and I would
baptize my lovers in honey.

Streetlights would flicker every time it rains,
orange hues sinking into bed with me.

Single-pane windows would frost up for me to leave my hand
mark behind.

Sweet smells of baked bread would tumble out of the window
across the street.
Steam gently grazing the cobblestone roads with crumbs
collectively feeding alabaster doves.

Here, heartbreak feels like picking woodland sage on a
luminous spring morning.
It would taste like hibiscus tea and fresh out the oven
shortbread cookies.

I would make Heaven my bitch

The Radium Girls

The Radium Girls were female factory workers who died of radiation poisoning from painting watch dials with self-luminous paint.

On these nights we gossip of our men

until the bosses say hush, and then we hunch

over watch dials, painting each number

into a radium glow, so that in midnights at the war

our men could see the time. The bosses tell us

to make our brushes a spear-tip

point on our lips. And so we spine the paintbrushes

into vertebrae. Then one girl whispers imagine,

what our husbands would say,

if we glowed, the way our lips would beg

for a kiss in the dark. Imagine, we could answer

 in light, not words, we could be chimera, tantalizing,

silent. So we paint our faces, flicker

as our flesh comes alive. We rename

our skeletons. Beauty is a debt

we pay from birth, our bodies servants

to their shadow. We paint until our nails scream

at the seams, shine until our secrets ash

between our lips. This is how a woman becomes

a mouth. Say this is how we're dangerous.

Say a husband's need could pierce our bodies

like sparks. Say he'll hold our ashes

in his fist.

Essay by
Husien Hammad

Mournings Start at Night

The shadow of a minaret brushed the old cobbled stones of Jerusalem as my new friends and I sat on a crumbling wall near the barbershop and hookah bar. Tourists were often lost and ended up on the Eastern Al-Qudz, where we made them feel wholly unwelcome. "Ingleezi, Ingleezi" we would shout, our throats still raw and new at 4 years old. This we would do for hours, watching one man drive away in a car that wasn't dirty white and rusting. White is a mourning color, and I suppose they hadn't heard the news yet. Everyone was mourning in Palestine, and everyone drove their sorrows on the streets.

Coming back many years later, walking past Al-Qudz to a vacant mosque, I see some boys shouting "Ingleezi" at me. It only took most of my life to walk along these down-beaten streets with down-beaten men.

***

My older cousin Hamza, after working as a Red Cross janitor, would sift through the trash in Western Jerusalem. We weren't hurting for money, but the Israelis seemed to be drowning in commodity, as Hamza brought my grandmother a collection of gold coins. She was a kind, powerful woman who controlled the home without compromise. She also was missing both canines and a front tooth, and with the coins went to the dentist who melted her new teeth.

Three things a Palestinian loves are gold, land, then family. Perhaps switch around gold and land, but family is a stoic and solid third. There is a violent infatuation with wealth, and Hamza would later go to prison for a year without trial or calling us after a dumpster-diving stint. He was a model citizen for two days when he came back. Then he took me to a dark-alley trade where he exchanged a parakeet for $300. We never owned a parakeet.

***

I had a best friend in the form of a rooster, who was living across from my house. The pen he stayed in was very much his, and his harem could have bested Suleiman the Magnificent's. He liked only *me* and was the peeve to everyone else in grandmother's home. My visits would last a few hours, and I would leave with small pecks on my cheek. He would always get mad when Uncle Abdullah would retrieve the hen's eggs. "Mine, mine" the rooster would shriek, running berserk at the wiry, white-haired man. Uncle would punt him across the paddock in return.

Later I would hear a pittering as I fed Roostie, his new moniker. He stood abruptly. He clucked slowly, wonderingly, then his throaty music would dull to silence. Analyzing. Then, an attack! Straight in the neck, he had killed a rat, blood dribbling onto his wattle. I was sure he was a monster at first because the rat looked so innocent and sweet in its death. Then behind it I saw more rats, eating freshly slain hens. The other hens heard the ruckus and went into the shed, and I ran away crying and screaming. I saw a war, but no battle was won, and the land was still contested between invaders and chickens.

***

A tragedy was playing on an Al-Bireh summer. The year 2003 was one where the *altilfaz* was airing the original *Tom and Jerry* in Arabic. Years later this misconception led me to ask a mute boy in America if he also spoke Arabic. Yet in that morning where the stranded clouds winked the rays, I saw it: a commercial for Campbell's Chicken Noodle Soup. I had never had it, so I asked my Uncle Abdullah if I could. He nodded, a tad confused, and took me outside to the chicken pen.

Next to the shed in the enclosure, there was a small wooden door and a rusted lock where a key once fit. The surrounding shack had rot in many places, so a good kick was much the same. Out came a congealed, rusted axe. And still naïve, I followed Abdullah to a tree stump where I sat during my meetings with Roostie. Speaking of which, I held his head down on the block, wondering in what way did we need these three things. An axe, a rooster, and a stump? Those things were alien with no pattern or consistency. Still more, my soft hands covered in the Mediterranean heat felt Roostie look a little left, a bit right, and finally to me. Right then I realized I had just damned him, as a *chunk* shuddered into my arms and blood caked under my fingertips. I ran across the street to my mother. She and Uncle Abdullah got into an argument, and he insisted. "That rooster was loud. I need to sleep past 6 a.m. We can get a quiet rooster next time."

We never got another Roostie, and even if we did, his meat would not have tasted as thick or been as sallow as my salted tears dribbled into the broth.

***

The market was old. Older than time, or the world, or even 1948, if you could believe it. It seemed to exist as one monolith, a bazaar so old you could call it the Bazaar, the Eye of the Silk Road, or the Place Where Your Marriage is Loudly Discussed Without Your Permission. Happily unaware of those future events that may or may not take place, the young me would walk from the light green scattered grass onto the Solomon-laid stone. I was told the ghosts of smokeless fire helped the Prophet set these roads, but what tobacco clouds had done was more grand to my eyes. The high arches would be cloaked in colored cloths like a pirate's sails, lined red and white, with spices and fresh breads or navy hovels in shady corners selling discs and CDs (most notably an Arabic *Tom & Jerry* disc).

My mother took my three sisters and me all throughout the lively outdoor mall. The girls seemed to have felt like three

Jesuses and this large archaic maze a single, benevolent king. They left with riches of sweets and toys and books and clothes. I only wanted one thing; a glow-in-the-dark ghost sticker. Doted on and filled with love, I cannot blame my sisters for forgetting or the joy my mother derived from my siblings, for the vacuous nature of a bazaar sucks you in. There is ceaseless potential in a land built in the shekel and dinar. But I left empty-handed and -hearted and sat forlorn and alone on the steps of the house. I was no Prophet in this story, nor a king of any fief. I felt like any of the boys who lived in Bethlehem, who watched the prodigy who argued with the rabbi in Hebrew win love and adulation.

***

Night is dinning in Palestine. Palestine is the sound of two hard stones skidding across the gray. In contrast, we call it *Felistine,* a word more beautiful and aesthetic. Cats love to run in the dark, to hunt for snacks and pettings where lamplights show shadows. They know it's Felistine. In the future, without asking them, an Israeli minister would propose deporting cats from Israel to another country. "Ridiculous, horrible," the Israeli population sounded in protest. "Cats belong here. They are a part of Israel."

I have an inquiry for all you cats out there. I do not believe that original sin is a justifiable argument, and you surely have a right to this land. But could you perhaps tell us of Palestine your secret? No offense, but you are house pets and street urchins, much like we. In Jerusalem I see cats warring in dark alleys; I see them run with doves from the sliding city Nablus with bleeding maws. You do what you must to breath 6,000-year-old air, much like we.

We live for this dirty air, just like you. So in the night when sounds are dangerous and fear chilling, come into our open doors and onto the flower-patterned floor tiles and whisper those secrets to us. You should tell that very young and bold me what I need to do, so in another time or dimension, I would know whether to stay, or to leave.

Washington Heights

You can't smile too much

in the hood.

You get a   *Yo, what's funny, b? I*
                             wanna laugh too.

                                      or

                        Wassup ma? I seen you smilin at
                        me, you trynna have a good time?

Nah, I'm good.

It's like . . .

I wanna leave the hood

but I'm scared if I go,

I'll lose the only home

I've ever known.

It's easier to *dream* in the

hood, my bro said

once you leave, you only dream

of coming right back.

When you close your eyes

you hear the street vendors

shoutin

COCO.MANGO.CHERRY

1 DOLLA 1 DOLLA

Anyone who grows up in the

hood has separation anxiety

We get a lil anxious if we

don't hear someone shout

YERRRRRRRRRRRRR

at least every 45 minutes

Fear&anxiety are handled

through scheduled fistfights

at Crackhead Park

We spend hours ballin our

home problems away til the

street lights turn on

all you hear is   *yo, we out to the bro's crib?*

We do anything not to go

to our own homes

We don't handle suicide

too well in the hood

we learn to go through

our hard times on the *low low*   but

to take our own lives?

That could neva

be at the top of the

list of resolutions

that's why when we hear

about these cases,   we.don't.know.how.to.act

We mourn them like they

were *our* blood   *because*

we know they felt like they ran out of options

& that shit hurts more than the notorious frosty

gust that sprints through our avenues   *Amsterdam Ave.*

                              is the brickest though.

We're from the Heights

where we keep candles

lit for the angles that were

taken from us too soon

We have guards in my hood.

Vivid murals of our street soldiers

who did not have a choice but to

become familiar with the streets.

Our little boys learn to make gun

shot sound effects by 2 & sag their

pants revealing the forest green&blue

plaid boxers their moms buy them by 5.

A Fresh White Wife Beater

Fresh Uncreased Timbs

Jeans

A durag

A fresh white t-shirt must be kept on the

left shoulder at all times.

I live to commemorate how we survive in Our Jungle. The Heights runs through my veins & I refuse to let it go on without me.

The Problem with the Fam

I like Sunday dinners
with the family
except maybe not with
my family

because . . .
how can I eat my
lasagna in peace
when I'm sitting at a
table with people who
once made me think God
made a mistake when
he put me

here? & I keep overexplaining
myself
*YOU DON'T OWE ANY
OF THESE PEOPLE AN
EXPLANATION*

but these *people*
are your family &
if your grandma heard
you talking like this, you
probably wouldn't have any
teeth left in your mouth, freka

but they make me feel . . .

not good
like I want to hide
in Tia Domitila's cold
ass room all Thanksgiving night
until mami finally finds me & says
Negra, let's go
We're leaving.

I wanna love
them so much . . .   I do.
But sometimes I think
the blood that runs through
my veins is not even close
to the blood that runs through
theirs

because . . .
I cry when I'm
angry
happy
hurt
shown affection
or looked at for more
than 3 seconds
AND THAT'S CONSIDERED WEAK
IN MY FAMILY AND THAT'S HOW
YOU GET LABELED LA LLORONA
AND I GET IT FROM MY MAMA,
THE O.G. LLORONA AND I'M
a gemini
AND THEY'RE ALL JUST A
BUNCH OF FUCKING
STRANGERS
sometimes.

Misunderstood
is the word all my therapists
   love to say,   "Your family makes you feel misunderstood . . ."
                                                          Yes, Daniel.
A part of me says
fuck em as I stick up my middle fingers *bothofum*
& the other side of me says
i love em
                     Again, I'm a gemini   THE gemini
                        And I'm tired of explaining
                        that N O we are not 2-faced
                         we just have 2 sides to us

                     I keep overexplaining myself.

Thoughts of Leaving My Casita

My bed is my sanctuary but
it lays under a roof that echoes
              t o x i c

                            How do I escape?
                      Can I bring my bed with me?
                   Maybe it's best to leave it behind

                         The memory foam layers
            keep mami's perfume locked in real tight

                   She *still* keeps a tight grip on my hair
                         ready to push my head down
                            the moment I disagree
                with her irrational nature that screams
                         "IT'S JUST THE WAY I AM
                        you either deal with it or
                              you deal with it"
                   At least I have an option, right?

                           How do I tell her my
         unhappiness does not = I want to leave her
                            by her lonesome
                     it means I require c h a n g e

Or I cannot stay
She never really prepared for this day &
neither did I
BFFs do not exist
for she is the only one
who once met my criteria to obtain this role
yet these past 3 years have been filled with
my 4-lettered name being yelled
as she stares up at the ceiling &
I can kinda see her uvula.
Never thought the day would come
where I don't want to hear my name anymore

aggressive Yeses & Noes

Resentment

Eye rolling

She prays for me to stop being such a *diabla*

Name calling

Laughter when triggered

Threats

I don't care

Dreams of being elsewhere

Journals filled with runny pages
where my words melt off the surface
                that has access to ishalanga's soul

                Guilt is still a lullaby she sings to me
            even when society has decided I am ready
                    to birth my own into this world
                        & sing my own lullabies
                    that are filled with anything else
                    anything else   but   guilt.

"Everything you can imagine is real"
- Pablo Picasso

"The Rats of the Paris opera house

scutter across the stage floors
limbs—longed and gawky:
a *petis de la rats.* Stage
rats infesting the opera in
a masquerade hidden under blue
tulle. Rats with pointed shoes
shaped like the speared snouted
head which sprouted ribbons that
twirled outward like the wispy
whiskers and scaled tails of
unwanted pests. Lurking

beyond the wings in shadowy
nests stalk men of every shape
and size in sexual unrest; hands
quiver in clamoring—capturing
the veracity of the real unwanted
guests. The ballet's notes singe
signaling the end and the begin
ning of the interlude and secret
private miglings of

the Pas de deux: a step of two
dancing together as if in mutual
creation. A supple back is arced
over in forced submission: the bend
ing of a *plié*—a tutu tulle pirouettes
out in plummets—pillowing softly
around knobby knees—falling over
pale skin til it spills around ankles
—sitting blue in the wings—patient
in fearful waiting—the exchange

of monetary pleasure. Bodies
knocking into one another in begin
ers frustration—the tip—tap—
touch of toes pointing down
ward—raising the head up
haloed in the stage lights
the last sense of innocence
crowned around the young girls
head faded into blackness as

the lights dimmed and the curtains
closed in the paris brothel house
Foyer de la danse : a night at the ballet

A Land That Will Not Sorrow
the Sadness

"There is no flag large enough to cover the shame of killing innocent people."— Howard Zinn

The Canary not   American   plumped

          wings plummeted perched to speak mended

shut   with barbwire   from   a   world

          who would rather

slit the black   birds throat and

          tear out one   of the Canaries bird

Box   than to admit   guilt

          to   the   shameless   slaughtering

"detox." All   sounds   songs   souls

        mimicked the monotonous melodious feigning

           of a   falsified nation

       who trapped   the

migrant birds who dare travel

       across the borders

       stole

their eggs hovering   hatching   birthing

       them as their own Damned creations

       eggs mothered by a land   who   could

never sorrow

their sadness.   Oh Great Green pheasant the   duped

enemy

dumped in "cages" scattered around   dusted   dried

     deserted

desert ground   Oh how I hear your cawing   in

the cebrals   of my mind.   The   mighty

thunderbird supernatural   suffers   a wobbled

wounded knee.   A massacre   masqueraded   in   the

            bellowing   buzzing

battle Trumpets   that provided   the   beat
that bathed the   birds, in blood of
mass

Extinction.   The american canary   with   yellowed

patriotic blissness   sings the

melodious   .   falsities of a nation borne
from   Silence

being forced feathered

down the beaks of every bird

            who wasn't

in the purity of

                  white.

Six feet away

from my loved ones

My family

My friends

My homeland

In this holy month of Ramadan

I am missing watching the sunsets
in overcrowded settings

Enhanced by the colors of different dresses
dancing with the sun's setting rays

I miss speaking in Arabic,
with distant relatives

Listing to them articulating every pronunciation
as they communicate their wisdom with me

My home is now empty of the sound of different accents
muzzled by the screeches of children's playing

They would clump together, even when they burst out running
Now they're more than six feet away

They have become distant like my family overseas
separated by miles of land and gushing seas

But today when I looked up at the moon
I saw that we are under one sky

The moon that I am looking at
is the same moon you see

This earth I inhabit
is the same one that future generations will

The gathering for iftar will be missing this year
along with the kind hands that welcomed me there

But this has been an opportunity for reflection

To cherish moments like these

Appreciate the overlooked blessing

in smaller settings

With the sun setting tonight

we will be reminded of the oneness of our community

That spans across oceans

and over borders

~~Trump 2020~~

As our hands are about to drag us over the finish line,

the possibility of another four years strikes us on the head with anxiety.

For those choosing a broken economy over public health, imagine you're forcibly stripped naked.

Expected to comply as if it takes the same ease as returning a smile to an old friend who is blind to your pleas.

Goosebumps conquer your skin as cold fingers trace your fists, your hardened shoulders, your lips . . .

Measuring tape caresses your chin slowly before wrapping itself around your throat.

They sit you down on a something cold to your naked ass and thighs and bombard you with 1in binders of palettes.

Which shade of oppression wears you best?

No one stops to ask you if you agree with the color choice . . . the shade. If you think it matters.

It is expected as if it isn't some newly written lie molded into truth with common sense, left to harden over centuries.

You're dressed in ill-fitting garments made of mismatched cloth and shoved onto a dimly lit runway.

The aged audience claps and you beg, "Is this who we are? Is this what we represent?"

Who are we when ideas are sewn into our skin?

Needle pulling threads of strung-up "alternative facts." Who are we?

When lies govern which air we breathe and what water quenches our thirst?

Who are we when our zip code determines the quality of our children's education and their likeliness to end up behind bars?

Who are we?

When self-love is a political statement?

When valuing your life is a political statement?

When fighting for clean water and air is a political statement? When marrying someone who looks like you is a political statement? When learning about where you come from is a political statement? When speaking your mother tongue is a political statement?

When asking for your unalienable rights is a political statement?

When your existence is a political statement?

When giving birth to yourself is a political statement?

When demanding safety from your institution of higher learning is a political statement?

Who are we?

When our children learn to associate skin to social caricatures before they have their home address memorized?

We are a nation shackled by apathy. And who are you?

You are history insisting on being a broken record at the expense of Posterity. Of Liberty. Of Justice. Of Freedom.

The oldest among us yet no wiser.

Essay by
Ruthie Carroll

Da Slockit Light

My grandfather died in the morning of October 28, 2017. I was away from home for the first time that fall, in my freshman year at university.

We knew he was dying. My dad had flown down to Fresno, California, to see him one last time. He stayed with my uncle, and they drove together to the old folks home. Dad had his fiddle with him, I know. He'd never travel without it.

I imagine the scene in my head countless ways, but eventually I muster the courage to make the phone call, a few years later, and ask my dad for his memories. He doesn't hesitate when I tell him what I want.

"He was a bag of bones," Dad tells me. "A skull with skin on it." My dad squeezed his father's hand. He says it could have been wishful thinking that the gesture was returned.

"I'm here to see you," Dad said. It's hard to know what else to say.

He played fiddle tunes to pass the time, but he doesn't remember which ones. Maybe some standards, maybe some of his own favorites. But "zippy," he tells me. At dance tempo. He wasn't going for any sad funeral songs.

The next day, Saturday, they went back to sit with my grandfather again, but they didn't stay long. It was hard, Dad tells me, to see his father like this, the way he doesn't want to remember. My aunt called, just as they arrived home, the first to share the news of their father's death.

* * *

I don't remember my dad's hair as anything but silver-gray and thinning. Looking at our old photo albums, though, I know I was alive when his hair was still thick and dark, like mine is now. I have so few memories from those early days— when Dad had more hair than me, and my parents still had a film camera—that aren't influenced from all the times I've looked through those albums.

In my favorite photos from my childhood, my dad is playing his fiddle. Our house is full of music from the day I am born. My ears know the sound from the moment I can look up and think, in my prelinguistic mind, *Listen to that*.

In one early shot, Dad plays sitting perched on a chair enclosed in a baby gate. My brother, maybe a year old, clings to the plastic walls, desperate to overcome this barrier and touch the music with his sticky fingers. If he weren't deterred by the two-foot fence, he would be hanging onto our dad's tapping feet and doing his toddler-best to mess up the old-time rhythm.

There are no pictures of me hanging outside a baby gate, but I'm not surprised. My mother was glad I didn't have the same exhausting curiosity for everything in the world. Even without a physical barrier, I imagine, maybe I knew we couldn't touch the music. After all, the fiddle carried my dad's notes outside the bounds of the fence whether we clung to the sides or not.

In another shot, all pretense of a baby gate is gone. I sit on my dad's knee as he plays, wearing my favorite dress, a Dorothy look-alike from the Wizard of Oz from last Halloween. When I picture this photo in my head, it's a sweet, playful moment between my father and me, marking the beginning of my love for fiddling. I must have looked proud and pleased to finally get up close to the music. When I find the real picture in an album, however, I have to laugh at this beginning. My chubby face is pinched in what looks like anguish: eyes shut, lips pouting. When I look again, I almost convince myself that this is a face of great concentration. Behind the camera, I'm sure, my mother is laughing at us both. As she focuses her 2003 film camera for the shot, my child-size hand is resting on my dad's bow arm so he can pull me into the music with him.

The next Christmas, my begging has paid off, and under the tree I find my very own fiddle—$1/16^{th}$ size, small enough to be a toy. My dad teaches me the simplest old-time fiddle tune he knows, "Boil Them Cabbage Down," but I play so rarely on my own. I still prefer to sit in my dad's lap, eyes shut, and let his arms do all the heavy lifting.

As I gradually learn to play my fiddle, I try to distinguish my own music from my dad's. This is my teenage rebellion, he jokes. Instead of the rhythm-driven Appalachian tunes he's fallen in with, I gravitate toward the complex dance melodies of Ireland and New England. He's not surprised, really. He used to play Irish mandolin himself, back in the day. I imagine the music lives deep somewhere, in the marrow of our bones.

One of my favorite people to play with is Skip, an Englishman whose eclectic knowledge of folk music gives me an idea of the kind of musician I want to be. Early in the evening at a friend's barn, we are trying to find tunes we both can play. Any genre is fair game: old-time, New England, Irish, Scottish, Québécois.

"Do you know this one?" I play him a snippet of something I've just learned. He shakes his head and furrows his brow in contemplation.

"Have you heard 'Da Slockit Light'?" he asks. I shake my head too. "It's slow," he says, "like an air. You can follow along."

The melody is at once haunting and homey, almost more of a slow march than a true air. I struggle through a few times, mostly just listening to Skip's fiddle sing. The first part moves in and out of the lower range of the instrument, and when the second part sits on the high string, I feel my breath rising to meet it. Skip slips into a harmony line and doesn't seem to mind that I can't recall the melody on my own. When we finish together, we nod in mutual satisfaction.

"What was that one called?" I ask. I need to write down the title and learn it for next time.

He has a copy of the sheet music in his fiddle case, so he gives it to me. "'Da Slockit Light.' It's a Shetland tune from Tom Anderson." Tom Anderson is one of the few famous Shetland fiddlers, as far as I know. At the bottom of the music, someone has printed an anecdote about the tune's origin from Tom himself:

> "I was coming out of Eshaness in late January 1969, the time was after 11 p.m., and I was looking back at the top of the hill leading out of the district. I saw so few lights compared to what I remembered when I was young. As I watched, the lights started going out one by one. That, coupled with the recent death of my late wife, made me think of the old word 'Slockit,' meaning a light that has gone out, and I think that was what inspired the tune."—*From a tape-recorded interview with Tom by a student in 1970. The second fiddle part was written by an American student in 1979.*

My mother and I take a road trip in the spring of my senior year in high school. We are touring universities in Oregon, then continuing south to visit my dad's family. It's wild to see California in April with all the flowers open wide that won't bloom in Washington until summer. My aunt gives us directions to the old folks home, and we arrive at a building that blends in with the rest of Fresno, a single-story complex with bland colors inside and out.

On the way to my grandfather's room, we pass a community gathering space with a big piano against the wall. I think for a moment that my grandfather would be there, sitting next to the instrument and listening to the guests and residents beat out their favorite songs. Grandpa liked almost all kinds of music, my dad tells me, except the window-rattling rock and roll he played in high school. Grandpa was a jazz man at heart, favoring old standards from when he was a kid in the 1930s—Coleman Hawkins and Ella Fitzgerald.

My grandfather isn't strong enough to get to the piano, though. We find him alone in his own little room. It's hard to tell if he's awake. His hospital bed is barely tilted up. A small vase of flowers sits on the side table; not the California poppies and lupine that are in bloom outside, but an unremarkable grocery store bouquet. The TV is on, tuned to a channel perpetually playing old black-and-white movies. My mother silently turns it off.

"Hi, Don." She knows how to compensate for hearing loss. "It's Amy and Ruthie." He blinks a few times, lost in the dim. "It's Amy and Ruthie. Forrest's wife and daughter; your son, Forrest."

"Oh, hello, yes." He looks behind me, and his eyes keep wandering the room.

"Forrest isn't here. He couldn't make it down this time," she apologizes. "He'll come visit you soon, though, we hope."

"Hi, Grandpa." I move a little closer and smile at this old man, a familiar shadow of the grandfather I remember from my childhood. The smile lasts a little too long, I think. I break the silence with the useless only question I can recall. "How are you doing?"

He doesn't hear my voice, so I set my fiddle down and crouch next to him. "How are you, Grandpa?"

"Oh, fine." Every word is a heavy rasp. "They're very nice."

I can only smile again in response. My mother eases words out of me, and I tell him about my school and our road trip so far. His attention wanders with my words, and I come to a stop.

"Do you want to hear some music?"

I unpack my fiddle and hold it under my chin to play an open note, not quite paying attention to whether it's in tune. I tuck it back under my arm. My mother and grandfather look at me, both expectant. This is my constant dilemma.

"What should I play?"

If Irish music is in my bones, it comes from my grandfather's DNA. His grandparents and great-grandparents were immigrants from Ireland and Scotland. My dad remembers his own grandma Ruth, my namesake, singing her Irish airs while she washed the dishes. My grandfather doesn't have a particular preference for fiddle music now, except to listen to his son and granddaughter.

I play him the standards that might still live deep in his memory. "The Irish Washerwoman." "The Butterfly Jig." "Little Beggarman." I reel out the notes in quick succession. Irish melodies can be eerie, but dance tunes aren't slow, somber affairs. I always become aware of how loud my fiddle can be when others are listening. The notes will carry beyond the thin walls around my grandfather, to strangers' ears. I am afraid I will disturb them.

Even in this shadowy state, I can see my grandfather smile. It's tiring to smile so much, though, and soon he's ready to close his eyes again. A nurse comes to check on him. She could hear the music from across the hall, she says. "Was it you? Beautiful."

My mother and I leave with goodbyes, my fiddle on my back. We don't know it yet, but we won't be surprised that this is the last time we see my grandfather. He already feels like a ghost of the old man I remember, light flickering in and out of memory.

Just before Christmas, Dad flies back to California with the rest of us—my mom, my brother, and me—for my grandfather's memorial. None of us are particularly happy to be travelling close to the holidays, but there's no other season when so many extended family have time off.

The day before Christmas Eve, we pile into a rental car and drive through the cold strip mall suburbs to the church. We don't wear black or stop my little relatives from running around the playground or really put on solemn faces ourselves. We're not that kind of family. The church is Unitarian anyway, home to the atheist humanism I was raised with.

As guests file into the folding-chair pews, Coleman Hawkins jazz standards play in the background. Next to the large Unitarian chalice on the back wall is a Christmas tree and a speaker's podium.

One of my young relatives lights the chalice candle to begin the service, and we sit in a collective moment of dedication. My three uncles and my aunt each stand to give their eulogies, as does one of my oldest cousins. I sit next to my dad. He is the quiet sibling in his family, another trait he passed on to me.

When our turn has nearly come in the order of service, my dad and I slip to the back of the hall to our fiddle cases, already unpacked. We are calm as we make our way to the stage, instruments in hand, and stand in front of the podium, next to the Christmas tree and the Unitarian chalice. Neither of us says a word. We lift our fiddles to our shoulders, exhale, inhale, and play for my grandfather "Da Slockit Light."

It's slow, like an air, but not a funeral dirge. Dad's harmony melds with my melody line, and we are one sound inside the hall. The repeated phrase that resolves the end of every part makes it feel like the tune could go on forever, but we play it only two or three times. There is applause when we finish, I'm sure, but I only remember my aunt and uncles who came to tell us afterward how beautiful the tune was.

At the end of the service, the chalice candle is extinguished. Everyone stays at the church for a reception: food, photographs, and more music among those with instruments. We alternate between old-time tunes, jazz standards, and Christmas carols, setting a festive mood for the rest of the gathering.

The next day we fly back to our own home and wake up after the whirlwind trip on Christmas morning. There's already a lot to remember around Christmas, and my grandfather isn't always at the front of my mind during the holidays. It's not the day before Christmas Eve that reminds me of him, or October 28th, or the California poppies that bloom in Washington summers.

I find him in the notes of "Da Slockit Light." He flickers in and out of the melody, somewhere between haunting and homey, a light only gone out until I pick up my fiddle and play the tune once more.

Poetry by
Meron Berhanu

የሃዜ

ዝለ

የሃዜ

የሃዜ

ፍጠር

ታሪክ

it is not my mother tongue –

ይደረሱ

ፍጠር

belitehali?

ደህና ሁን
ደህና ሁን
ና ሁን
ሁን   መገንባት

በት

belitehali?

— but how my mother speaks to me

With my K!

With my K! and my T! T! I whisper some

before I sleep to see if my mouth

 still remembers how. How to K! and T! T!

(Like k'ēsi and tilanitina.

k'eyi and tenanekegn)

I fall asleep and but my lips do not,

beating restlessly through the night,

K!'s and T!'s T!'s

Story by
Shreya Vikram

Empire without a Timeline

We are in the car when Father starts to tell me about Ma. She was never like this, he says. She was the softest person I knew. So thin, you could hardly see her and so quiet, you couldn't hear her when she spoke. I had to force her to speak up.

I think of Ma, shy and slim and silent, cloaked in flowing white robes like a dead goddess. Disgust wells up in me. I choke it down. We say nothing for a while. He catches my eye in the mirror.

But even then, he says, she had her obsessions. Like her teeth. She would never talk before she brushed her teeth, wouldn't even let me near her. When she did brush, she had to do it before a clock, counting each second. Two minutes. It was just one of those things. I teased her about it often, even though I found it odd. I should have known.

Sneak into Father's room, my feet whispering across the tile floor. A mattress, old and sagging, laid on the floor. Father sleeps there, snoring steadily, his hand thrown over the smaller outline of my brother. Used to be me who slept there. He'd hug me until I fell asleep, promising to never leave, but I always knew when he shifted. I'd watch him as he walked to my mother's room at midnight. At first, I'd call him out on it, angry and sobbing. I never understood why he'd have to sleep with her when he had me. It felt like a betrayal, to watch him stumble across the sofa, knock softly on the door, my mother pulling him in. He hated her. I was all he had. Later, I learned to settle.

Watching the slow movement of their chests as they sleep, I kneel on the floor, open the cupboard, and find the album. I touch it, and my fingertips come back covered in dust. In the dark, something scrambles across the cover. I stand up, search for a duster, then shove it into the cupboard, shaking it wildly over the book. Spiders crawl out, barely visible. I jump, then wince at the sound of my falling. I hold my breath, but the steady rumble of their snoring continues. Crawling across the floor, I near the cupboard again, take out the album, keeping it as far from my body as possible, and sneak back into my room.

On my bed, I flip through photo after photo. The first few pages are of their marriage. Ma is startlingly thin, her collarbones jutting out in a way that frightens me. Her cheeks curve in, gaunt, as if she'd been starving herself. One photo zooms in on the couple holding hands, and I notice how the bones in her wrist protrude. When they close in on her face, her nose is elegant, shapely, curving upward at the tip. I wish I'd gotten her nose. I've gotten Father's instead, which is flat and resembles a pig's. I smooth a hand over her eyes, as if closing them.

I first see this album when I am ten. I ask her why she's so sad in the pictures. All brides are sad, she says, because you enter a new life, but you leave an old one. I had to leave my parents for my husband. I remember her saying this, but I can't see the shape of her face or her body. I don't know how she's sitting, whether I'm curled up in her lap, whether she smoothes a hand over my hair and holds me close. Is it even her that says it? Or is it Father, trying to explain Ma's sadness to a ten-year-old daughter, pressing his lips to my hair as we rock from one side to another. When is the last time I spoke to her? I cannot remember. Sitting there in the dark, my hand trembles, then steadies. I consider keeping the album back but cannot bear to. I hide it under my bed instead, then sleep uneasily, dreaming of children with sugar-high blood, light as feathers as they leap into their mothers' sad wedded laps.

*

From left: Ma's father, Father, Ma, Ma's mother.

They stand stiff and happy on the altar. Ma's small finger is curled around Father's as they swear their oaths. Her face is thin. Serious. Kajal on his eyes, smeared heavily. I'm thinking of the eggs, the day when she takes me with her to the flea market to buy 180 eggs. Exactly. I feel like a spy as I count, first the rows and then the columns, nine and ten, with two plates, my body trembling as I multiply, quick, before she shoves them in her bag, and we walk back. Later I tell grandma. A hundred and eighty? she asks. Are you sure? I nod, something sinking in my stomach. Father stands there, looking worried. I know I have disappointed him, somehow, by not keeping these secrets. I never speak of Ma to anyone else again. It's hard to imagine though that this is the woman who once locked her sobbing 5-year old daughter up in a house alone as she left for god knows where. I lean close to the page, then press my lips to hers. She tastes of ash and dust.

In the car, we talk again. How did it happen? I ask. When did it start? She stopped sleeping, he says. She would toss all night, unable to calm down. I tried everything. I gave her spiced hot milk, played music, turned the AC down as much as she wanted, until it was so cold I could hardly breathe. I stayed up with her all night when she still couldn't sleep. Nothing worked. She would walk through the day with no rest, slow to respond, quick to anger and tears. Once the teachers in the school she worked in found her sobbing in the bathroom. I asked why, but she couldn't say. That's when she stopped working too. There was nothing left for her. She sat at home, locked herself up. Withdrew.

*

In the summer of tenth grade, I shift schools. The new one is private, expensive. I attend on a scholarship. I don't remember when it started. At first, I try. I text in the chat room. Join in on classroom discussions. Stay around for breakfast and lunch and eat with everyone else and laugh whenever they laugh. I don't remember when I stop trying, only that I do. It is so easy, too. So natural. I hate the kids. One is depressed, diagnosed bipolar. She uses me as a punching bag, and I let her. The others are rich; they drink and smoke and don't know what it means to work. Quickly, I become the class nerd. It is so easy. All I have to do is stop trying. Stay in myself.

Once I go straight to the library after arriving at school, then stay there until the bell rings for class. When it is time, I pack my books and carry my backpack up to homeroom. Two sets of staircases, then fifty-two steps down the corridor. At the fiftieth step, I stop. Think of what it would be like to walk into class with my backpack on while everyone else is sprawled across the seats, snickering to themselves. I consider leaving my bag here, sneaking into class, pretending I've been in the restroom all along. I consider hiding my bag just outside of class and darting in at the last minute so there'd be no time for anyone to wonder where I've been. A group of boys pass me, so I fall to the ground immediately, pretending to rummage through my books. When I can no longer hear them, I sit. Kneel in the corridor, unmoving. All of a sudden, I want to cry. No one, absolutely no one is around.

*

From left: Ma, me, my cousin, Father.

Where is this? A beach. California. The skies are so blue they hurt my eyes. Sand everywhere, covering my shorts, my hair. I am 8, maybe 6. My hair in pigtails. Sticking out straight, like black twigs. Ma is thin, not as thin as she was in the wedding photo, but still thin. She is smiling, shy. Father says she never liked taking photos. She never liked any attention at all. She stands behind us, unprepared, not posing, as if she'd been rushed in at the last moment. Father is thin as well, and young. So young. It's hard seeing him like this. Unworried. Did he know what would happen? Had things already started then? I look to her face. Scan her eyes for signs of madness. They are clear. Unassuming. When did she know she'd fallen? When did she know?

*

Soon, I can't sleep at night. If I tell Father, he'll scream at me for not eating enough and then shove more food down my throat, so I do nothing. The hunger isn't the problem. I can take the hunger. This is something else, the sleeplessness. It has a new quality to it. A desperation of sorts.

One night, after hours of tossing, I decide it is too hot. I need the AC. I reach my hand out and pat around the pillow for the remote. Nothing. Sighing, I scramble up, switch the light on.

For the next three hours, I search for the remote. As each second passes, I sense a fear growing inside me. I am convinced I need to find this remote, there is no way around it. My gut turns, twists, twisting, I turn the house over, throwing the clothes to the floor, the books, wandering from room to room in the dark, my hands fumbling for the switches.

I wonder whether I am dreaming or hallucinating, whether I even exist, whether I have dreamt myself and this room and this dark and now, can't find the part of me that exists apart from the dream, lost too much of myself to myself, gave too much—a wave of fear overcomes me. I collapse to the tiled floor and tuck my head into my chest, curled tight. I feel hands in the dark. Long and unyielding, groping at my skin, and a rage, so sudden and sharp, I could scream. I sob instead.

*

The next morning, I wake up in my bed. At first, there is the disoriented calm. The rapid blinking of the eyes. My hands fumbling at my limbs as if making sure all of me is still present. I stretch and feel a tightness in my back and neck.

In the bathroom, I scrape my tongue first. When I spit, blood is mixed in with the grime. I watch the red swirl down the drain. Then I brush my teeth, taking my brush with me to the hall, where I stand in front of the clock. Two minutes start with the second hand at 15. Thirty seconds in, I wander. My memories come to me in a flood. First the slow coolness of water, then the pulling away, seductive, drawing me in, further, further, then the sudden, mistakable sense of drowning. I freeze. One minute, forty-five. I keep brushing. Paste drips onto my shirt, and I wipe it away with my thumb. At two minutes, I go back to the bathroom to spit. I am rinsing my mouth when the hair on my arms prickles. The lid of the toilet bowl is open an inch, dark pooling around the gap. I know it is silly, but I can't bring myself to close it. Beside me, my loofah swings softly on the hook. I set a single foot outside the washroom, and then another, then slam the door behind me as hard as I can. Outside, I heave and heave.

*

From left: Father, me, Ma. This is a recent one, taken maybe two years ago. The year I start starving myself. No one has noticed then: In this photo, I am still fat, though I can see that I've started to shrink. Already, my eyes are clearer. A few months later, people will notice, and there'll be an uproar in the family. Especially my aunt, who wants to be my mother. The girl who forgot how to eat, she says. What are her parents doing? So much shame. I stop talking to them then. Father is the only one who sticks around. In the photo, Ma too has shrunk. She too is starving herself. She is not as good at it as I am. This brings me immense joy.

Yesterday, she walks into my room, locks the door, and sits down on the bed. I am writing. I think of her sneaking into my cupboard the week before to read my diary and then throw it out. She never admits it, but the book is missing, and she's the only one who'd have taken it. A few hours later, she tells me to stop keeping the diaries. People are cunning, she says. They're always going to compare their life to yours. You can think about your life, just don't write it down. I say nothing, just stare at her and leave. I complain to Father, and he says he'll talk to her. I don't think he'll do anything.

Now, she sits on my bed, jerking her head to the sides as she takes in everything. I don't look up. She touches my cheek. I flinch. Suddenly, she speaks. Do you know of any way I can lose weight? she asks. Her English is broken and unfamiliar. I look up, not making eye contact. Disgust wells in me, flecked with a strange panic, then spite. If you'd been better at starving yourself, I want to say, then you wouldn't be asking.

No, I say. I don't.

I just need to get this off me, she says, gesturing to her body. I've grown too big. Tell me about a diet. Anything I can do.

This is girl talk. Maybe any mother would do this. Maybe this is normal. I sit there, feeling, suddenly, as though I am choking. Just one month ago, I have given up the starving. Black spots, lightheadedness, hair loss, brittle nails, an unwavering sense that I am going to die. The last one scares me. Despite everything, I do not want to die. Hair trigger. I breathe, in and out.

No, I say. I don't know anything.

I'm just asking. Desperation leaks into her voice. Drip by drip.

I look down and pretend to type. I have work, I say. She stays a few minutes more, her eyes burning into me. Then stands up and leaves.

*

Night. The car again. I make casual conversation, then wind us back to where we started. Father doesn't resist. She stopped talking to people too, he says, after that. She couldn't bear them. Thought they were all plotting against her, trying to bring her down. The paranoia was the hardest. She'd tell me things she thought she'd heard, seen. It felt real. She was so convinced. I didn't know what to do, so I broke off connections with everyone. It was just me and her against the world.

He pauses here, lost. Then: and even that didn't last. I asked her to see a doctor. She thought I was trying to push her in. Said I was abusive. When she did see the doctors, they never stopped giving me second looks. The police stopped us once on the way to the hospital. She'd been beating herself up. Just throwing herself against the wall. They looked at her, the bruises on her forehead, her arms. They took everything in and didn't say a word. Just stopped us. I had to tell them she wasn't well. It took three doctors and two hours to convince them.

A bike swerves in front of us, cutting sharp. The car jerks to a halt, then moves on, Father cursing under his breath.

It's a woman's world out there, he says.

*

The hunger is killing me. I toss in my bed until 1 a.m., and then give up. I walk to the kitchen, but there is nothing to eat. I go back, try to sleep again. I feel wide awake but exhausted. My eyes are burning, begging to close, but it feels like someone has pinned them open with clothespins.

At 2 a.m., I give in. I walk to Father's room, but he isn't there. Only my brother sleeps, alone, already learning to settle. Ma's room is locked. I will have to knock, risk waking both of them up. Ma is unpredictable. If she gets upset, Father will never treat me the same way again. My knuckles hover over wood. I try knocking but can't bring myself to do it. Five times I try, five times I give up. The sixth, the softest tap. I listen for sounds of shuffling. Nothing.

I consider my choices: If they have already woken, then the damage has been done. If they haven't, I can either try again or give up. I stand there in the dark, thinking of Father raging out, furious at me for waking up Ma, then decide it isn't worth it. I turn, my stomach still rumbling, to go back to bed, maybe read for the rest of the night. Or pace up and down the hall.

Might burn an extra 200 calories if I walk fast enough. On my fifth step, I hear the shuffling. I feel a sudden panic, then relief. Nothing can be done now. There is more shuffling, some murmuring, then the click of the lock giving way. The door swings open.

Father stands there, his face red, panicked, as if he expects me to tell him someone has broken into the house. When he speaks, his voice comes out cracking at the edges, heavy with sleep. What happened, he asks, several times. I try to calm him down. Dread pools deep in my belly. I try to keep my eyes as cloudless as possible. I'm hungry, I say. That's all. He breathes. Once, twice. Shuts his eyes tight. Then explodes toward the kitchen, his steps harsh and unforgiving. I flinch, already regretting this, already hating myself. Should have slept. Should have been stronger than this.

He takes out a plate from the rack, dusts off cobwebs. My stomach turns at the thought of eating off the unwashed plate, but I say nothing. He slams the plate on the table, then goes inside the kitchen. The table is smeared with last week's leftovers. Chewed leaves, whole pepper, spilled rice, gravy, all caked and dried. I sit down. A cockroach scurries out from beneath my plate. I swallow bile, forcing myself to stay. He returns with rice. Piles it onto my plate. Frantically, I calculate calories, maybe two cups on the plate, so 412, 450 to be safe, then another 100 for the ghee, 550, then 400 for the gravy, absolutely not. Absolutely not. He says nothing, only stares. Cockroaches scurry at the end of the table, dancing nearer and nearer. He looks at them, then slams his hand down, crushing one. I close my eyes. Bile rises in my throat.

Eat, he says. You're hungry, aren't you? I nod, then force a handful into my mouth. Swallow. When a cockroach scurries too close, I am almost relieved as I take my plate away. I can't, I say. He stares. Then he stalks into his room and brings out a bottle of repellant. Sprays it all over the table. The smell is overpowering. Poison. I try not to breathe, not to look as the roaches run frantically over the table, a few running toward my plate, then collapsing on their backs, white liquid oozing out as they die. I look up at him, but he doesn't seem to notice. Eat, he says. Why won't you eat? He stands there, towering over my plate. I feel a sharp disgust in my throat, choking me as I shove another handful of rice into my mouth.

*

From left: Ma, me. Just the two of us. We are sitting on a swing. A long one, the kind where a plank of wood is strung up from the ceiling so it hangs flat a few meters above the floor. Ma's hand is swung around my shoulder. She presses me close to her. In this photo, she is properly fat, possibly the fattest she's ever been. Flesh hangs off her in chunks. She wears an ugly green sweater and a scarf, even though it is June.

When did she stop seeing, stop feeling? Stop tasting, too. Father says her food used to be perfect, now it's barely edible. Of all the things, this upsets him most. Later, she'll walk up to us and say, the food was great today, wasn't it? I can never meet her eyes. I scan my face for signs of discomfort. Did I love her then? Do I remember loving her? I don't, but I wish I did. I remember the odd things, like when she screamed at me for petting a dog. Didn't I know all dogs were ghosts? They'd eat me right up. When I go sobbing to Father, she denies it, saying I must have been mistaken, it was my aunt who said this. Stupid aunt. We're never letting her into the house again, okay, darling? She pats my head and holds me close. I am so confused.

*

The hunger again. Why can't I be stronger than this? Why am I so weak? I toss in my bed, sleepless, exhausted. At 1 a.m., I am digging in the fridge. I can't turn on the light because Father is still working. A late-night meeting. I find something that feels like a box of grapes, then whisk it into my room. I place it on my lap and eat in the darkness. They are so sweet. I hate myself with every bite. Every so often, I touch something that feels soggier than usual, and I avoid those grapes and eat around them.

When I come to the end, I notice that the skin of my pants are soaked. The smell of something sweet, in a decayed sort of way. Shuffling outside, sudden and without warning. I hide the grapes underneath my bed and pretend dead. The cloth sticks to my thighs. Something is wrong. More shuffling, louder now. Then the light. Blinding. Father. Are you asleep, he asks. Calls my name. Twice. I watch him through my eyelashes. My body stiff. Aching. Can't pretend any longer. Stretch, then blink heavily, as if waking from a deep sleep.

Why is the light on, I ask, my voice thick. He looks at me oddly. Shame, tugging at my flesh. I want to curl up in a corner and disappear. He knows. He says nothing. Then leaves. My hands and thighs are sticky. My skin starts to itch. I wait, unmoving. Listen. Five minutes pass, maybe ten. No shuffling.

I crawl off the bed, then turn on the light. Take off my pants first, then wash up, trying to get the stickiness off my skin. When I take the box of grapes in my hands again, I see it. Worms. Hundreds of them. The grapes decaying at the edges, purple with mold. Bitten. The worms crawling, so small. Juice drips down my hands. I drop the box, then rush to the toilet, heaving.

*

The laughter came last, he says. The car again, night again. These long drives have become the only places we can talk with no fear, no hatred.

That was after the medication, he says. She'd go through cycles of emotion, sinking so low none of us could reach her, and then floating so high, she lost touch with the world. There was never a balance. We tried to keep her in the highs. The lows were dangerous. She cried all the time. We never knew when she'd try something. Constant surveillance. I suppose that's why I can deal with the laughter right now. We've been through so much worse.

I think of Ma in the restaurant yesterday, wearing clothes far too tight for her with no bra and a white-and-pink scarf meant for 3 year olds. Cream spills onto her chin and neck as she eats, chewing with her mouth open. She laughs like that too, shaking, spilling more food onto herself. Father and I look down at our own plates and pretend everything's okay.

When I ask to take a bite out of his sandwich, father shakes his head silently. The last time she'd snapped back. No, she said, her eyes sharp. There's spit in that. It's disgusting. Don't ever share food again. When I protested, she started screaming, spittle everywhere, that Father was trying to seduce me. We stopped trying then. Sitting in the restaurant, all of us eating alone as if no one else existed, her eyes razor sharp on my plate, moving cutlery around for a better view, making sure I don't do anything that'll offend her, even as she laughed and spoke and gestured to the voices in her head. I feel a sudden rush of hatred for her. When we walk back to the car, she tries touching me, tries to sling an arm over my shoulder, around my waist, laughing again, tears spilling from her eyes from the force of her laughter. I could slap her.

Laughter's good for you, isn't it? Father asks. That's what I tell myself. At least she's happy.

*

Soon, I can't sleep alone at all. I wake up often in the middle of the night. I go to the kitchen to get something to eat. One night, I walk in, turn on the light, and nearly scream. She clamps her hand over my mouth and whispers, her voice raspy as a smoker's, her naked body pressed into mine. Her skin like a snake's, soft and scaly. Shh, she says. They're listening. I nod twice, two nervous jerks of the head. She holds me for a moment longer, then lets me go.

I stand there gasping for a second, then turn, shaking. I open the fridge and grab a cup of yogurt. I watch her out of the corner of my eye as I open it. She arranges nine onions, three in a row, on the counter. She asks me to pass the knife. The edge glints as I give it to her, my hand trembling. She takes it, her eyes flickering over me as if I'm not there. I am overcome with an urge to turn around and check to see whether there is anyone behind me, but I don't want to take my eyes off her. My eyes water as she cuts the onions. I wince with each chop.

Once she is done, she puts them in the mixer, and grinds them into a paste. Then she smears it over her hair. Halfway through, she turns. Blinking as if seeing me for the first time, she asks me if I want anything. I shake my head and walk softly to my room.

In bed, I think of us, standing in the kitchen together past midnight, mother and daughter, tiptoeing around and whispering as if doing something illicit. I feel a sudden rush of affection for her, then fear.

*

From left: My aunt, my cousin, me, Father, Ma. My aunt's house. A festival, or maybe just the weekend. Ma and Father are visiting. They stand awkwardly, like strangers. I'm standing with my cousin, who's pressed against my aunt. If this weren't my family, I'd think my cousin and I are my aunt's children. In a way, we are. I almost grow up there, for the first ten years of my life. Go back—sobbing each time—to my parents' house for the weekends.

Once, when I refuse to eat—and this is before the starving—my aunt dumps the food onto my head, drags me to the bathroom, and scrubs the rice and gravy into my scalp as I sob. This is what I remember of her. But that's unfair. She tries, as much as she can. Each time she gets my cousin a dress or a necklace, she hands me one too. But it is always deliberate, as if to say, you're my daughter too. Only you'd never say that to a real daughter. I am no one's daughter, and I know it. She knows it. I stop talking to her after the starving. Stop talking to the cousin too. My aunt comes up to me later at a wedding. She grips my shoulders and says, I treated you like a daughter. I treated you like a daughter, and this, this is what I get back. Nothing. Her fingers burn into my collarbones. She looks at me with disgust. Her eyes are so red.

*

Once, when I am 10, father and I are walking along the railway when he ruffles my hair and tells me I'm going to grow up to be my aunt, my mother. All girls do, he says. In this memory, he kneels in front of me and looks me in the eye. They're all selfish and cunning. Sweet little girls grow to become hard, mean women. I look at him, angry, then throw my arms around him. I say, I hate you or don't say that or I won't or I don't want to grow up. He holds me tight and says, they all do.

We don't talk for the rest of the day. The next morning, he asks me if I want coffee, and I say yes. He never apologizes, and I never bring it up.

*

The talking starts slowly. At first, it is in my head, a single tiny voice that spirals into two, then three, then an entire new universe, one where anything is possible, where I can live through every single one of my fantasies with close to no effort. It is so easy. Feels so real too. I read once that the one thing that separates humans from animals is our ability to simulate the future, to experience, in its full richness, a landscape that we have never lived through before.

Sweet irony then, that it is the same richness of imagination that leads me to my madness. Lying in bed in the dark, my mouth moves speechlessly, my hands making secret gestures in response to the shadows that save me from my loneliness. They are fluid, creatures of necessity, pouring themselves into whatever I need them to be. At 1 a.m., exhausted, I lie there, paralyzed by a sudden fear. How I have scorned her for her weakness, which is now becoming mine?

*

From left: Ma, me. Another with just the two of us. I am older here, maybe 12 or 13. Already I am showing visible signs of discomfort. In the picture, I have angled my body so no inch of my skin touches hers, and we stand there completely apart, the sliver of distance aching wide between us. Was this when I had stopped trying? Was this when I left the fear for apathy, for disgust, for hatred? I remember the fear so well: that night when father tells me to sleep beside ma, for just one night, and I lay there, to please him, my eyes wide awake, body trembling as she shakes beside me in a noiseless laughter. Sometimes she would turn, her movements sharp and sudden, get up, and start talking, still soundlessly, her hands making meaningless gestures. In the dark, I shut my eyes and pretend to be dead.

*

Night, I tiptoe to Ma's room. Crack open the door. Father walks up to Ma. Ma is fat, so fat I can't make out her features from behind the layers and layers of flesh on her face. He takes her hands in his, edges close, and says, you fucking bitch. What sort of a curse have I gotten for a daughter? What have you done to us? We were happy before you. Leave your mother alone. I stand behind them, or maybe above or below—no sense of direction in this dreamscape. I say, she's not your daughter, I am. I say, why do you keep confusing us? I say, I'm not her. Thin now. Look at me. Look at me.

*

From left: Father, me. There's so rarely a picture with the two of us, especially after the starving. This one was taken maybe two years ago. I wonder where. We almost never spent time together. Why? What happened? I can't remember. Was it the laughing? The talking? When he walks into my room and finds me with my head cocked, speaking to the walls, my lips spread wide into a smile. I flash back immediately, but the damage is done. And the crying too. At first, it is reasonable. At the slightest provocation, it comes up, tears thick and heavy, but I can will them away and dig them deep. Soon I learn to default my expressions, to switch back to a smile whenever I'm not deliberately controlling the movement of my face. Smiling is always appropriate. When my friend tells me she broke up with her boyfriend, I keep smiling. She never talks to me again.

Later, I can't stop it. The tears flood out. I am leaking. Leaking salt. The skin on my cheeks is dried paper, and salt water drips down them. Two holes where there should have been eyes. I sob as I wake up, and I sob as I brush my teeth. I sob more once I realize there is no way to stop the sobbing. When Father sees me, he clenches his teeth and leaves. Standing there in the middle of the room, all alone, I sob harder. My sadness is a living thing. I feel possessed. Father walks in again, and I try to stop, but my breath heaves, and the tears flow. He digs his fingers into my shoulders. Bone on bone. I wince through my tears. What do you have to cry about? he says. He looks at me, his eyes hard. I say, I thought you would understand, or how could you do this to me? or what is wrong with me? or nothing. I wrench free, curl up in my bed, and sob some more.

*

The car. Drive to my aunt's house. I am still sobbing, hardly able to breathe. Sometimes I think I will die. I feel very, very sick. The car is closed. My sobbing fills the air and chokes me. I can see it now, its thick grayness. Like liquid smoke. I open the windows and heave. We say nothing.

We reach the house. I beg him not to take me in. He stands there, his eyes red. We are both possessed by the things we dug our graves for. Him in his rage and me in my sadness. We swallowed the bones and held them deep within us, but they crawled out. The body as a pipe, holding nothing. All of a sudden, I want to die. It is a profound feeling.

We walk inside. My aunt sees me, flinches, disgust, alarm, rage, concern. In that order. I feel weak and collapse at the doorway. Distantly, I hear Father say nothing's wrong. Just take her in. I laugh, or try to. I sob again.

I hear whispers.

I remember flashes.

I cannot tell apart the present and the past.

Father walks/walked me out, tells/told me not to make a fool of myself. I sob/sobbed in the street. People watch/watched. Father says/said, you're just like her. Father says/said, she was like this too. Wanted all the attention. Father says/said, you've ruined my life. Both of you.

Essay by
Sophie Braxton

Girl with Broken Shoes

I consider my shoes mine. I consider the damage a form of realization. I consider it a washing away of society's hold—a baptism by the soiled water of my own self.

The shoes in question are canvas and rubber, their soles specked with recycled compounds of once-used product. They are remarkably broken. To others, they might bring to mind our scant modern art—thrown together *with intention,* meekly joyous, defiant.[1] To me, they are instead reminiscent of an idealistic understanding come into direct contact with Truth. Or maybe the shoes could represent the Truth—mutilated by those who don't like it.

They don't call their own shoes unbroken—that would be redundant, they think, because shoes *should* be unbroken. Mine bear the defining prefix. Mine demand an explanation.

---

[1] Anything that deviates from the standard is described as "defiant", whether or not its intention is to defy.

The broken shoes matter to my managers under the premise that they matter to the customer. They matter to my parents under the same premise—that other people will perceive me as somehow lacking, which will in turn reflect badly on them.

The open mouths of my shoes are said to speak grotesque amounts of evil regardless of whether I can hear it. The propriety actions are secondary only to the asepsis of my shoes. All sins would puncture and deflate at the sharpness of a toe.

A lady offers me $20 with which to buy new shoes. She wants to bless me, she says. Her hands are shaking, a peace sign necklace dangling between her breasts. As I consider her, an uncomfortable silence accumulates between us. I tell her that I like my shoes. "I'm sure you do!" she emphasizes. "Buy ice cream then. I just want to bless you." $20 is too much to buy ice cream and too little to buy shoes. I thank her and take the money. There is nothing else I can do.

My dad laughs. My mom laughs. My grandparents laugh. I am an island of sincerity surrounded by undulating disdain. They find my sock beneath the broken layers. "I can see your sock!" they say, like a sock is a secret.

"It looks horrible. It looks like you don't care."

"I bet the corporate people come in and go to your store managers and say, 'Hey, there's a homeless person in your backroom!'"

I am never told to care,[2] I realize, but to *present* myself as a Person Who Cares.

Under a similar doctrine, my manager says that as long as we have balloons, the store can be a mess, and everything can be out of stock. After a day, the balloons deflate, and the latex hangs empty and sad. We step over those wrinkled carcasses and find ourselves tangled in ribbon.

I remember trying to surrender myself to Jesus as we were told to do. I was 9, and my Bible was illustrated with cartoon people. White people wearing purple robes. The instructions on how to surrender were unclear, so I asked for clarification. "You just have to believe," they told me. I had gone to church my whole life. I had stood when told to stand. I had held hands with wilting strangers. I had stared into the light of an artificially twinkling electric candle.[3]

All that time, I later discovered, my parents had never actually believed in God—and still they drove us to church. They sent me to Sunday school.

---

[2] Actually, I'm supposed to care less about my current job as a clerk at a grocery store. Everybody wants more for me—thinks I deserve more. *More what?* is the question that should naturally follow, but never does.

[3] We switched from real to electric candles during the singing portion of the Christmas Eve service because of the *risk of fire.* It occurs to me that the risk is not of *fire,* because there had always been fire, but of *uncontrollable* fire.

Once I learned what *surrender* meant, I decided that surrendering was not a good idea.

Sometimes it is difficult for me to believe that humans are vertebrates. My manager tells someone else that he is afraid to talk to me about my shoes. He attempts to discreetly find out my shoe size. He must find perfection titillating. I imagine his walls lined with framed photographs of Things That Are Not Broken—things unknowing, but unquestioned.

Some virtue is that of grafted trees—uniform rows of pretty saplings, sprayed with pesticide to keep the uglier aspects of life at bay.[4] Some springs untrue from the seed and grows honest over years. It is a question worth considering, whether one is more valuable than the other.

The boy's eyes are watching my shoe. The boy looks tired. He might be 6. I wonder if he has already tried to surrender. I wonder what he has been told, and how much of it he has taken for Truth.

---

[4] Apples do not come true from the seed (an apple tree planted from the seed of a Honeycrisp apple would yield sour fruits of a completely new, likely inedible, variety), so the only way to grow a certain type of apple is to graft saplings, a technique by which orchards of clone trees are created. The lack of genetic variety makes them very susceptible to infection and calls for an increased amount of pesticide.

"Why are your shoes broken?" he asks.

"I like them that way," I say, choosing a ready defense over the more honest answer, *they broke*.

"Really?"

His dad puts a hand on his shoulder and pulls the boy closer, embarrassed. The boy smiles a shark smile, so many teeth.

When people say they do not like children, I question their logic. Children are people who have not yet learned to live by the script of expectation. No adult has ever asked me why without the intention of laughing at my response—it is a joke for which I am expected to supply the punch line. Their insults are implied under an excess of niceties. Their questions are just statements, asking for agreement.

"Shouldn't you get some new shoes?"

"Don't you think your managers wish you'd wear some reasonable shoes?"

Reasonable is a funny word for such a statement. The notion that You Should Not Wear Broken Shoes to Work falls under the umbrella of common sense, but common sense is not sense at all—it is only common. Such ideas are believed to be beyond explanation, removing the necessity of reason. This is how people become what they are without noticing what they are becoming.

My mom doesn't like to wear hats because she feels like everybody is noticing her hat. If you were wearing a hat that you like, I wonder, wouldn't you want people to notice it? But yes—a hat might change the name of your portrait from "Woman" to "Woman with Hat."

From my broken shoes, so much is assumed. Sometimes I wish I could obtain the imagination of the public and stomp on it like one would do to extinguish the beginnings of an uncontrollable fire.

Imagine the same portrait, a woman with a hat, but titled "Woman with Horse." There is no horse, but rather than questioning the title of the piece, everyone gets close and squints. They point to shapes in the background, wondering, *Is this the horse? Is this it? Maybe—maybe she's sitting* on top *of the horse.*

Some things are subject to examination while the inculpability of other things is simply assumed.

Eventually the searchers will find some vague figure that passes, through desperate eyes, for a horse.

I wear different shoes when we go somewhere fancy. The reason is this—affluent people who are very high up will look even downer on me for wearing broken shoes, which will reflect even badlyer on my parents. The shoes are my sister's. They are brown, too big, and have holes in the bottom, where the damage is not visible but more consequential, because water comes in even when the ground is only damp.

It feels like lying to wear those shoes—the closed toes jutting forward and mumbling bureaucratically so you can't exactly make out the words, but it sounds like something you'd agree with completely.

Our new manager has a Russian accent. I think it would be nice to have an accent—whatever you say, it is yours, and it could not have come from anyone else. When people repeat what she has said to them, even just informatively, they half-heartedly imitate her voice. I can tell whether they are paraphrasing.

"Can I speak to you?" she asks me. "In private?" I nod.

We go to her office, and she closes the door behind us. Managers come and go, very different people, but the office does not change in appearance. What looks like paperwork is hung on the walls.

She tells me to sit down, and I do. She says that she loves me.

She has only worked here for two months, and she already loves me as a person,[5] and she wants to buy me shoes. "Can I do that for you?"

I shake my head. I know I am smiling, and I wonder how she is interoperating that smile. My shoes are tucked underneath the office chair, and my socks touch the floor. I

---

[5] Because I am sweet. The word that has been consistently used to describe me throughout my life is "sweet." Only when people look down at my shoes do they feel inclined to describe me as "defiant" or "stubborn."

wonder briefly if this is a gentle kind of verbal warning and whether it will go in my file.

She continues to ask, and I continue to say no. She's smiling. I didn't think she was pretty at first, but kindness has decorated her face—Woman with Generous Smile. We have been staring at each other for a number of minutes, and I wonder what she thinks of my eyes.

In grade school, my friend insisted that brown eyes were boring until one day a trick of the light made them golden and she decided they were pretty. The victory I felt was unreasonable. It occurs to me now that my eyes had not changed since she insulted them, so it must have been the light that garnered her praise.

I used to tilt my head, searching for that pious moment when the sun would pollute my eyes with its excess and make me Girl with Golden Eyes. *I like your hair*, the same friend said. *You should straighten it.*

The most cinematic argument I have ever witnessed occurred in a produce cooler in the backroom of my store. A man and a woman shouted at each other, arms moving angrily. Their words traveled coldly on visible breaths. As I watched them, the structural integrity of the building we stood in was called into question. How does anything stand that has been built by the hands of such equivocal animals?

In the backroom, they screamed and threw boxes,[6] but on the sales floor they spoke brightly of lemons and eggplants. To me, they were kind, but to each other, they were formidable. I think they would have stopped arguing if they had seen me watching, but I grew wary of the intimacy I was witnessing and walked away, my shoes making noises like Jesus's sandals on the ground.

I have tried many times to see myself as others do, but it is impossible. Subliminally, like everyone, I hide my flaws and present only what I see as virtue—but someone can never hide a thing so well that they themselves do not know where it is.

Even grafted trees, even titled portraits, carry reverberations of a discordant cacophony—whatever dissatisfaction led to their creation. I look at my shoes, and I see material quite like us, fighting to be free of its function.

Our store manager is cheating on his wife with the assistant manager, Woman with Generous Smile.[7] My friend

---

[6] Later, during a fit of anger, Woman with Visible Breath closed a sliding door on her foot and broke it.

[7] This accusation may or may not be true. They were allegedly "caught" in the office by a coworker at the store where they both used to work. When he was asked to leave that store (partly because of the allegations), he brought her with him as assistant manager. It is widely accepted as truth, and I am

told me that. *I didn't tell you sooner,* he said, *because I know things like that make you sad.* (Earlier, he tried recapping a fistfight between cashiers for me, and I covered my ears. What made someone so gentle[8] become Woman with Fist-Shaped Hands?) *It's been going on for a long time. Most people know about it. You know she followed him to our store.* I nodded, remembering her unfaltering smile as she offered me shoes. *But corporate won't fire them because there's no real proof.* She had been nervous to ask the question, and I had been nervous to hear it. Afterward, we hugged.

And now I know that she plays a sordid part in a larger and uglier world.

Maybe to say that the world or its people are ugly is unfair.

In school, we wrote poems about disfigured things in a way that made them seem beautiful, and my sister chose my shoes.

The shoes are like a map of time
With rips and holes along the lines
The shoes are like a holy shrine
Of some god, somewhere, undefined

---

inclined to believe it, based on what I know and what I have seen.

[8] Instead of her legal name, the cashier was called Harmony Bliss. She made her own name tag and wore it over the one they give us.

I think rather than ugly, indifferent is a better description of our world, and ambivalent a better word for us. Some people wear different shoes, and different faces, every week. What I see as a lack of structural integrity may still be faithful to the intention of the architect. I don't know—I haven't seen their plans. My shoes are hugged by thick black tape. Woman with Generous Smile still smiles, and just as generously.

Driving home, I remember crying at the Truth. *There she is,* people might say—the people who offer me things I don't want—*the girl with broken shoes. And she's crying because she doesn't have money for new ones.*

What Are You Doing This Quarantine?

I'm not planting a sabal palm in my backyard. I'm just sitting here. Eating. I'm scrolling through canceled flights as I look outside with sarcasm all over my face. I'm leveling out a cup of flour and putting it in a bowl. Doodling squiggles in my bullet journal before I close it. I'm flying . . . paper airplanes. I'm gonna yank out one of my molars later. I just bought a life-size Totoro plush online. Tonight I'm making a bronze cast of my dog's paw. I've decided to put up a fence just in case. I've decided to become an astronaut. *hold on* Peeing. Now I'm painting on my makeup. I've decided to glue googly eyes onto the back of my head. I'm checking the Guinness site to see who holds the record for unraveling a toilet paper roll. Questioning how Metta World Peace feels about world peace. Memorizing and forgetting all the bones in the human body. Staring at a wall. Slicing a coconut open with a katana. Sketching a blueprint for a new tree house. Researching the horse that looks like a unicorn. Grazing. Planning a jousting match for this horse. Eating fried rice while humming to the theme song of *Friends*. Watching Animal Planet while I wait for the coffee to kick in. Deciding if I should dress up as a rancher or an equestrian next Halloween. By the power of Greyskull, I have the power. I thunder. Thundercats, Hoooo!

Unintimate

With your fingers inside me

I am at my most

pitiful.

My coarseness grates against

the smooth, sweating skin

just above your collarbone.

I am not the one

that deserves to feel

your gasped breaths against

my jaw or to caress the

grooves between each rib

below your breast.

I don't know what you expect from me.

As my pelvis tilts up

toward your touch

my consciousness slithers back

into the dimmest corner of skull.

Damp and writhing,

its terrified

moans seep out

among the rest.

I should be watching

multicolored stars

dart across the inside of my eyelids,

Instead,

my focus is on the cowlick

at the edge of your hairline

and the wet smack of our lips.

I'm afraid that when we're done

you will hold me

and whisper that you love me.

At 83

what if at eighty-three, all i had was a little house in Charlotte, arthritis in my joints, and a photograph of the love of my life

what if my last taste of success was eons ago, in the midst of cities with cars that sounded like ocean waves, roaring and rushing past me

in the flash of white teeth smiles, i had seen luminescent visions of fame

my own name in black-inked newspapers

champagne in backyard pools

and this was my destiny—my life's purpose

i knew it, tasted it, and still wasn't enough to uproot the universe

i

. . . wasn't enough to uproot the universe.

what if i had spent my entire life crawling, climbing and killing only to find myself—

in a little house in Charlotte, arthritis in my joints, and a photograph of the love of my life to find myself drowning in black tar, watching ghosts flit in and out with the breeze, old friends with red lipstick, cigarettes between their fingers

my daughter getting ready for her dance recital—

unable to let go?

Story by
Brooke Stanicki

Moths

It was dusk, around the time that moths usually flutter into the ambulance. They float over the stretcher and smack their little bodies into the synthetic light of the cabin bulbs. Normally, it is my job to kill them. But the radio was quiet that shift, so the ambulance doors stayed shut until nearly 11 p.m. The squad room smelled of alcohol wipes. A cop show rerun played on the 20-year-old television.

"Rig-3-13-Ryder-Road-Room-112-for-the-75-year-old-female." The dispatcher's speech was pressured, the familiar rhythm of abject exhaustion and over-caffeination. I looked at my radio and waited for the next line. It squawked again. "For the pandemic." I got up from the couch—its cushions had been used so much that they were molded in the shape of an ass. My partner remained still, dirty boots still on, flat on the adjacent couch. I nudged his shoulder.

"I'm awake." He stayed still, brim of his beat-up 2008 Kickball Champions baseball cap pulled down over his eyebrows.

"Then get up."

"Fine."

I walked into the empty street toward the passenger side of the ambulance. My partner knows I don't drive. That's a lie; I do drive. Only in emergencies. When the patient is closer to death than life, when it's time for all hands on deck. Except my hands. In emergencies, I have the youngest hands. They are the first to be shooed away. They are the first to be handed the keys. Then I drive.

But this wasn't an emergency. Because the patient was alive—at least alive enough that we hadn't been told otherwise. So I didn't drive.

My partner pulled the rig out of the parking lot, nearly flattening a poorly manicured bush in the squad house landscaping. I didn't comment when I usually would—I knew how tired he was. The city was zombie-movie quiet, the kind of quiet that was inherently suspicious. But such quiet was getting more normal by the day. We entered an empty highway. I counted the streetlights until I lost count and started again.

"You got this one?" he asked.

"Mhmm," I grunted.

We exited off the highway and entered a local suburb where the grass was always yellow. I wondered who was doing the lawn care, if anyone at all. A group of deer picked at some sickly brown strands on the side of the road. Without warning, my partner moved his hand to the inside console and turned on the siren.

WHOOP WHOOP WHOOP

"WHAT THE FUCK ARE YOU DOING?"

"I am moving the deer."

"They weren't even close to us."

"Well, now they're gone."

We turned another corner. No need for navigation on this call. The Excelsior Nursing Home had been our most popular caller for months. To be fair, they had that honor before this point too. But it was different now; things were more fatal. Frequent flyers didn't call any more.

My partner honked at a Buick blocking our way. The driver extended a meaty hand out of the window and flipped us the bird before driving out of the parking lot and into the night. My partner turned on the radio, some old rock that my dad would have liked. I pulled a pair of small gloves from my pockets and shoved them onto my sweaty hands. They stuck to my palms, to my fingers. I ripped the left hand. I replaced it with another.

"Yuh good?" my partner asked.

"Yeah" I responded.

I slipped a pale yellow gown over my arms, tying it in a bow at my neck and waist. I covered my surgical mask with a bulky N-95 respirator, so big that it invaded my line of sight and covered my whole chin. The department had run out of small-sized masks three days ago. I slipped a face shield behind my ears, the plastic hitting me lightly in the nose. I pulled the stretcher out of the ambulance and started pushing it toward the Excelsior's large wooden doors. I waved to my partner. He grinned and flipped me the bird.

I was stopped at the lobby by the receptionist, who looked panicked. I assumed she was a new hire. The nursing home doctor looked angry as he approached. Angry about his job? About missing an early tee time tomorrow? About the world and its rejection of science? Maybe angry about everything, maybe angry about nothing. I nodded my head and anticipated a report.

"Closest hospital," he said. He pushed a stack of medical records into my gloves, looked at me, and walked out. I nearly laughed out loud. Great report.

A nurse was already wheeling a bony little woman toward me. She was sitting in her wheelchair, nasal cannula tucked neatly into her nostrils. The nurse, a Black woman in her 40s, wore a disgruntled expression and Tweety Bird scrubs. I considered complimenting her scrubs, but figured it wasn't the time. I grabbed the patient's brittle shoulders, covered by a woolen shawl. The nurse grabbed her ankles. "1, 2, 3," I counted. We lifted her from her chair to the stretcher. I wheeled her outside, raised the stretcher, and slid her into the ambulance. I hopped in the back, closing the doors behind me.

"HELLO, CAN YOU TELL ME YOUR NAME?" I asked, shouting through my layers of personal protective equipment.

"I can't," she paused to cough, "hear you."

"YOUR NAME?" I repeated.

"My name," she gasped, "is Jean." Another pause, another cough. "And I know who the president is so you don't have to ask."

"THAT'S A GOOD SIGN," I responded. I replaced Jean's nasal cannula with a mask, providing her with high-flow oxygen. My radio squawked again. The paramedics, who had been dispatched to our location, were being diverted to another call. I started taking Jean's vitals, slowly inflating a child-sized blood pressure cuff around her little arm.

"DO YOU HAVE ANY CHILDREN?" I yelled. Old people love youth.

"Can't hear." She coughed, violently this time.

"I-I WAS JUST ASKING IF YOU LIKED MY OUTFIT," I joked, mostly to myself. I continued my assessment.

A few minutes later, she pulled off the oxygen mask to speak. "It doesn't compliment your figure." I laughed so hard that my face shield slipped down my forehead. I pushed it back up.

"LET'S GET YOU BETTER," I said, holding one of her porcelain hands in my sweaty purple gloves. She smiled at me the way you smile at a child who wants ice cream for breakfast.

Upon arrival at the hospital, a nurse greeted us, wheeling a freshly made hospital bed into the cool night air of the ambulance parking lot. "You got this," I leaned in and told Jean as I had told so many patients before her. I am a big fan of hope in all its forms, including hope without cause for hope, hope based on whim, hope based on luck. I even settle for false hope.

I climbed back into the ambulance to decontaminate. A confused moth flew aimlessly, smacking its wings into the overhead lights. I was feeling optimistic. I let it live. We took calls until the blurry sunlight of 6 a.m. rose over the city, obscured by clouds of smog. Day laborers wearing dirty surgical masks wandered the empty streets as I drove home to sleep.

A few nights later, I was back on the couch, watching the clock tick past midnight. I heard a police officer radio the paramedics to confirm a time of death. It was Jean's room number. In the darkness of the squad room, in the ass-shaped depression caused by many EMTs who had sat there before me, as my partner snored lightly, I cried for yet another person I didn't know.

Essay by
Surina Venkat

To the Previous Generation: Thank You

We inherited a world on fire.

That was the thought that ran laps in my head on the first day of 2020. We'd settled down for breakfast when my sister surfaced from Instagram, eyes wide. Australia's burning, I remember her saying. That day the thought was literal: A continent was aflame. And it was the result of years of adults—people in power, people like you—ignoring climate change and downplaying the issue. I grew angry that this was the world my generation had to deal with: How were we supposed to fix this?

And as the year went on and the coronavirus spread within the United States, I grew even angrier. The pandemic brought to light so many inequalities in our society by showing us who had access to electronics, who had money for rent—and who didn't have to worry about any of these things. And when George Floyd died on May 25, leading to a long-overdue racial reckoning in which we began to unearth centuries of targeted oppression and discrimination, my anger at the previous generation reached its boiling point.

"We have to fix all your generation's mistakes," I snapped at my father one night.

His response left me speechless because it revealed an angle I had never considered. "You think we didn't try to fix them?" he asked.

The question threw me, and later when I thought about that moment, I felt ashamed. Because in my anger, I had forgotten one important detail: You fought as hard as we did.

I know my history, but sometimes I forget it. Sometimes I forget it was you who demonstrated in the Stonewall Riots in 1969, paving the way for LGBT+ rights. Sometimes I forget that it was you who organized marches for the Civil Rights movement in the 1950s and '60s, striking down countless racist policies and practices.

Sometimes I forget to be grateful for the people who fought and died for our movements, who dedicated their lives to making a difference. I forget to be grateful for people like Marsha P. Johnson, Grace Lee Boggs, Martin Luther King Jr., Sylvia Rivera, Ida B. Wells, Kamaladevi Chattopadhyay, Lala Lajpat Rai, Rosa Parks, John Lewis. I forget to be grateful for the countless other people who made these movements, who fought selflessly for change without ever reaching for glory. And that makes me feel ashamed because without them, we would not be where we are today. To say that what they did—what you did—doesn't matter to me and to blame you for where we are right now disrespects your sacrifices and hard-won victories.

Sometimes I forget I would not be in this country without you. My parents are immigrants; if you hadn't forced Congress to get rid of the Asian Exclusion Act, they wouldn't have been allowed to live here. I forget that I owe my life to you, for all the fights you undertook, the wars you waged and won, just so my generation could get to where we are today.

And where we are today might not be perfect: There is a lot of unaddressed inequality in our communities, our workplaces, our schools. Our homes. But we've come a long way because of you, even if we haven't gone far enough.

"You stand on the shoulders of giants," my father told me. And he was right. Because of the brave people who came before us—because of people like you—we can go farther, run faster, and soar higher than ever before. If we touch the clouds, it's because you built us the ladder. If we bust through buildings and tear down ancient structures, it's because you handed us the wrecking ball.

So thank you. Thank you for giving us a chance to reach higher than you did. The battle for our planet and its people won't be easy—realizing this is what made me so angry in the first place. But if there's one thing I've learned from watching you all fight, it's that together we have the chance to make a difference. And, at the very least, we can make our world better for the people who come next.

Editors

Emma Harrington (she/her) is a 20-year-old junior at Hamline University. She is pursuing an English major with a focus in creative writing and a gender and women's studies minor. Emma is currently the collaborations programmer for Hamline University Programming Board  and editor-in-chief of Hamline's literary and art publication, *Fulcrum Journal*, in which she has been published twice. In addition, Emma will have poems in the upcoming issues of *Emery's Online Journal* and *december* magazine. In 2016, she was a National Student Poet Finalist. Outside of poetry, Emma enjoys bike rides, gardening, and watching movies with her four wonderful roommates.

Originally from suburban Eagan, Minnesota, **Abby Doty** is a 21-year-old college student attending Hamline University in St. Paul, Minnesota. She keeps herself busy on campus, despite the pandemic. She is currently an editor for Flexible Press, the  managing editor for *The Fulcrum* at Hamline, and president of Hamline's Psi Chi. She's still figuring out her future plans as a double major in psychology and English, but currently enjoys her free time by reading, writing, and petting dogs.

Madelaine Formica is a 23-year-old who graduated in spring 2020 from Hamline University with a BFA in creative writing. Her passion is fantasy writing, and she has been published in *Daily Science Fiction,* an online literary journal for flash fiction. This summer she moved from  Virginia to St. Paul to soak up the literary life that the Twin Cities has to offer and start a position at Secuarian Financial as a customer service rep. When not writing or working, she can be found planning road trips or curled up watching way too many movies. She is excited to have helped share the creative and thoughtful voices of those 22 and under through this journal and encourages others to have a voice when they may feel overlooked because of their age.

Kayla Gray holds an AFA in creative writing from Normandale Community College and a BA in creative writing from Metropolitan State University. Kayla lives in Minneapolis and is usually found writing young adult fiction.

Contributors

Rose-Marie Athiley (she/her/hers) is a senior at Hamline University in Saint Paul, Minnesota, where she studies English and communication. Rose-Marie moved to the United States in 2006 and through learning her third language found the art of the pen and word. Her love for poetry has found itself in her academic essays and newspaper articles. Rose-Marie uses her poems and essays to foster empathy and understanding.

Meron Berhanu is a first-year MA creative writing student navigating the cultural spaces of being a first-generation British citizen with an Ethiopian heritage. She explores how poetry can be not only a linguistic medium to equip minority communities with a voice but a visual medium too. Descended from an Ethiopian heritage and a family of refugees, she poses the question of how oral history can use poetry to make this past not only visual but incarnate. Breaking the rules of poetry's traditional form and lineation is both a poetic and political statement in refusing to conform to the doctrine of the cannon, infamous for excluding or falsely representing Black communities.

Richard Bowman has been a writer since he first learned how to put sentences together. He is an advocate for the Black community and a critic with the firm belief that it's necessary to work for change in society and his community simultaneously. He's lived in Indianapolis, Indiana, his entire life, and Naptown is where he first found his voice as a writer. His writing is blunt, honest, and unapologetic. He strives to push the envelope with his writing and open the space for commentary on issues that others may not be willing to discuss.

Sophie Braxton is 19 and lives in Decatur, Georgia, where she works and writes. Her work has been published in *Into the Void*, *The Southampton Review*, and *Thin Air* magazine.

Megan Brooks writes historical poems, tragedy and loss, and political poetry and prose. Born and raised in Virginia, Meg is still attending school in the area. She is an upcoming graduate at the University of Richmond, majoring in leadership study and minoring in creative writing and English. After starting as a business major, she quickly learned that the lifestyle wanted nothing to do with her and she with it. She found she preferred making her own path through writing her own stories with poetry and switched her entire track (five times). Megan has recently been published in her school magazine, won an award from the Academy of American Poets, and is now featured in Flexible Press. To learn more about Megan, go to

https://mbrooks791.wixsite.com/serendeptioussparrow"
https://mbrooks791.wixsite.com/serendeptioussparrow
or email her at Mbrooks@richmond.edu.

Ruthie Carroll is from Seattle, Washington, and studies creative writing and web content development at Western Washington University. She primarily writes fiction, but she has begun to see the value in true stories as well. Her writing has been published in *Jeopardy* magazine.

Steviee Geagan (he/him) is an emerging writer born and raised all around the Western Pennsylvania area. He has been published in *Pulp.*, a literary journal, and *The Siren*, and was a finalist in the Roadrunner Review's 2019 writing contest. When Steviee isn't reading submissions for BatCat Press or Pulp., he desperately pleads with his well-loved Mr. Coffee to brew enough joe to last the night.

Husien Hammad is a multifaceted writer and editor-in-chief for his university newspaper. With work that ranges from poetry and political articles to satire, all he really lacks is validation of the quality of his work. Originating from an American-Palestinian family, his personal goals are thoroughly looked down upon, and his parents hope dearly his job requires wearing a suit. Instead, he hopes he can craft a story that can keep you invested.

Jareeaa's two worlds intersect at her identity. She is a college student learning how to navigate the world. She is a Syrian-Muslim-American who loves to explore her surroundings. She is studying to become a doctor and is actively engaged with her community.

Mary Kelly (she/her) was born in Wellington, New Zealand, and now resides in Vancouver, Canada. Having just completed her first year at the University of British Columbia, she hopes to continue her journey into writing poetry. Focusing on topics such as mental illness, love, and adulthood, she dissects the world around her and curates poems applicable to different lives.

Kevin Kong is a Chinese American student from the Southeast. His creative work has been recognized by the

Scholastic Art and Writing Awards and Poetry Society of the UK.

R.T. Lundquist has been working on novels and writing short stories for years, but although she loves composing things, she can never quite seem to finish anything. Short stories are easier to let go of, and one of her stories was published in the *Penultimate Peanut* magazine in April 2020, and another published with *The Book Smuggler's Den* in July 2020.

Owen Matthews is a junior in the Princeton University Politics Department, pursuing certificates in East Asian studies and journalism. She grew up in New Jersey and genuinely believes it is the best state. Before college, Owen spent a year living in southwestern China and is fluent in Mandarin. In summer 2020, she interned at SupChina, writing stories on Chinese business, culture, and politics. In her free time, Owen enjoys performing improv comedy, running, and writing creative nonfiction pieces. During her freshman year of college, she took a travel writing course with Pico Iyer and has been hooked ever since. She is thankful to everyone at *22 Under 22* for putting together this great collection!

Uma Menon is a 17-year-old author from Winter Park, Florida. Her debut book, *Hands for Language*, was released by Mawenzi House in 2020. She is the 2019–2020 Youth Fellow for the International Human Rights Art Festival and attends Princeton University. Read more at theumamenon.com.

Anna Pasno (she/her/hers) Anna, a Filipino-American, was born and raised in a small town in Wisconsin. She's passionate about coffee, social justice, food, and of course, reading and writing. After her graduation from the University of St. Thomas in 2021, Anna hopes to work in the Twin Cities' rich and diverse publishing industry. Between the ages of 12 and 15, Anna wrote and self-published three YA novels, and the Summit Avenue Review has published three of her works over the last two years: a poem, "Lilies for the Maid of Orleans" (2019), a creative nonfiction essay, "Tampo" (2019), and a short story, "Petals to Butterflies" (2020).

Gaia Rajan (she/her) lives in Andover, Massachusetts. She's the managing editor of *The Courant* and the poetry editor for *Saffron Lit*. Her work has appeared or is forthcoming in *DIALOGIST*, *Rust + Moth*, *Hobart*, *Kissing Dynamite*, and elsewhere. She is a 2020 National Student Poet semifinalist, and her chapbook, *Moth Funerals*, is forthcoming from Glass Poetry Press. She is 16 years old.

RJ Robertson-DeGraaff is an emerging queer poet whose work has been included in *GNU Journal* and Seven Circle Press. He is an undergraduate student at Western Michigan University, majoring in creative writing.

Isha S. Serrano is a New York-based Afro Latina poet. She records her authentic visions, dreams, and daily experiences in her poetry. Isha received the 2020 honorable mention for the Grace C. Croff Memorial Prize for Poetry. She has been a lifelong writer and began journaling in the second grade, which eventually led to her finding her true love, poetry.

Brooke Stanicki (she/her/hers) is a new writer with published fiction and poetry. She has been featured in Indolent Book's "What Rough Beast" poetry series and has fiction in *The Syndrome* magazine and in the anthology *Tymes Goe By Turnes* by Arcane Publishing. When not writing, she is a pre-med student at Johns Hopkins University in Baltimore, Maryland.

Surina Venkat (she/her) is a 16-year-old writer and activist from West Melbourne, Florida. She has work published or forthcoming in *Cast of Wonders*, *Ayaskala Literary Magazine*, and numerous anthologies. When she isn't reading or writing, you can find her running with her dog or listening to her newest podcast obsession.

Shreya Vikram is a writer and artist based in India. She is the recipient of the Dorothy West Scholarship 2020. Her work is forthcoming in *Cobalt Review*, *Ruminate*, *GHLL*, *Salmon Creek Journal*, and elsewhere. You can find more of her writing at shreyavikram.com.

Yoko Zhu is a 17-year-old from the Atlanta, Georgia, area. She identifies as female and uses she/her pronouns. This is her first anthropology feature, but she's been published in *JUST POETRY!!!*, which features high school poets. Yoko occasionally writes on the back of napkins or in between the lines of a spare notebook; it's typically a chaotic mess. Besides writing prose and poems, she enjoys painting and educating herself on politics. She has aspirations of becoming a journalist.

Cover artists

Chad Lowther is a poet, writer, editor, artist, and librarian. He resides in Cleveland Heights, Ohio, with his cat, aptly named Alizon Device. His score for a poetic performance entitled "Flowers at Morning" was published in *Barzakh Magazine.* Furthermore, "A Little Love Meditation" was published in *Drunken Boat,* now known as *Anomaly.* His short story, "The Immutables," was published in the 2013 *Anthology of Crack the Spine.*

Bob McNeil, writer, editor, spoken word artist, and illustrator, is the author of *Verses of Realness*. Hal Sirowitz, a Queens poet laureate, called the book "A fantastic trip through the mind of a poet who doesn't flinch at the truth." Among Bob's recent accomplishments, he found working on *Lyrics of Mature Hearts* to be a humbling experience because of the anthology's talented contributors. Copies of that collection are available at https://amzn.to/3bU8Loi.

Home: An Anthology

A collection of Minnesota-focused short stories, memoir, and poetry: exploring hope and loss, promises kept and promises broken, in their own personal search for home.

Lake Street Stories

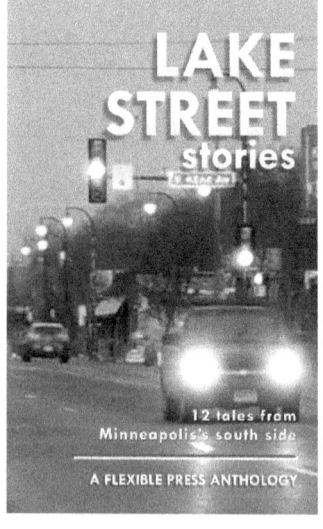

An anthology of 12 short stories by Twin Cities authors, exploring themes of struggle and rebirth, immigration and social change, and community and challenges, all focused on south Minneapolis's main street.